CONTENTS

June 24, 2002

HOMELAND SECURITY: THE FEDERAL AND NEW YORK RESPONSE

MONDAY, JUNE 24, 2002

HOUSE OF REPRESENTATIVES,
COMMITTEE ON SCIENCE,
Washington, DC.

COMMITTEE ON SCIENCE
U.S. HOUSE OF REPRESENTATIVES
WASHINGTON, DC 20515

Hearing on

Homeland Security: The Federal and New York Response
Monday, June 24, 2002
9:00 a.m. – 12:00 p.m.
Utica College, Utica, New York

WITNESS LIST

Panel I

Dr. John H. Marburger
Science Advisor to the President
Director, White House Office of Science and Technology Policy
Washington, D.C.

Mr. John S. Tritak
Director
White House Critical Infrastructure Assurance Office (CIAO)
Washington, D.C.

Dr. James Engle
Deputy Undersecretary for Science and Technology
United States Air Force
Arlington, Virginia

Mr. James K. Kallstrom
Special Advisor to the Governor
New York State Office of Public Security
Albany, New York

Panel II

Mr. Robert Weaver
Deputy Special Agent-in-Charge, New York Field Office;
Director, New York Electronic Crimes Task Force
United States Secret Service
New York, New York

Dr. Yakov Shamash
Dean of Engineering
State University of New York at Stony Brook
Stony Brook, New York

Mr. Michael Miravalle
President & CEO Dolphin Technologies, Inc.
Rome, New York

HOMELAND SECURITY: THE FEDERAL AND NEW YORK RESPONSE

FIELD HEARING

BEFORE THE

COMMITTEE ON SCIENCE
HOUSE OF REPRESENTATIVES

ONE HUNDRED SEVENTH CONGRESS

SECOND SESSION

JUNE 24, 2002

Serial No. 107–71

Printed for the use of the Committee on Science

Available via the World Wide Web: http://www.house.gov/science

U.S. GOVERNMENT PRINTING OFFICE

80–337PS WASHINGTON : 2003

For sale by the Superintendent of Documents, U.S. Government Printing Office
Internet: bookstore.gpo.gov Phone: toll free (866) 512–1800; DC area (202) 512–1800
Fax: (202) 512–2250 Mail: Stop SSOP, Washington, DC 20402–0001

COMMITTEE ON SCIENCE

HON. SHERWOOD L. BOEHLERT, New York, *Chairman*

LAMAR S. SMITH, Texas
CONSTANCE A. MORELLA, Maryland
CHRISTOPHER SHAYS, Connecticut
CURT WELDON, Pennsylvania
DANA ROHRABACHER, California
JOE BARTON, Texas
KEN CALVERT, California
NICK SMITH, Michigan
ROSCOE G. BARTLETT, Maryland
VERNON J. EHLERS, Michigan
DAVE WELDON, Florida
GIL GUTKNECHT, Minnesota
CHRIS CANNON, Utah
GEORGE R. NETHERCUTT, JR., Washington
FRANK D. LUCAS, Oklahoma
GARY G. MILLER, California
JUDY BIGGERT, Illinois
WAYNE T. GILCHREST, Maryland
W. TODD AKIN, Missouri
TIMOTHY V. JOHNSON, Illinois
FELIX J. GRUCCI, JR., New York
MELISSA A. HART, Pennsylvania
JOHN SULLIVAN, Oklahoma

RALPH M. HALL, Texas
BART GORDON, Tennessee
JERRY F. COSTELLO, Illinois
JAMES A. BARCIA, Michigan
EDDIE BERNICE JOHNSON, Texas
LYNN C. WOOLSEY, California
LYNN N. RIVERS, Michigan
ZOE LOFGREN, California
SHEILA JACKSON LEE, Texas
BOB ETHERIDGE, North Carolina
NICK LAMPSON, Texas
JOHN B. LARSON, Connecticut
MARK UDALL, Colorado
DAVID WU, Oregon
ANTHONY D. WEINER, New York
BRIAN BAIRD, Washington
JOSEPH M. HOEFFEL, Pennsylvania
JOE BACA, California
JIM MATHESON, Utah
STEVE ISRAEL, New York
DENNIS MOORE, Kansas
MICHAEL M. HONDA, California

HEARING CHARTER

COMMITTEE ON SCIENCE
U.S. HOUSE OF REPRESENTATIVES

Homeland Security: The Federal and New York Response

MONDAY, JUNE 24, 2002
9:00 A.M.–12:00 P.M.
STREBEL HALL STUDENT CENTER
UTICA COLLEGE
UTICA, NEW YORK

1. Purpose

On Monday, June 24, 2002 at 9:00 a.m. the House Committee on Science will hold the third in a series of hearings examining the vulnerability of our nation's computer infrastructure as well as research and education challenges and opportunities facing the Nation's network security infrastructure and management. The Committee will also examine the connections between the Nation's science and technology enterprise and U.S. law enforcement and other first responders in the fight against cyber terrorism.

2. Background

The terrorist attacks of September 11, 2001 brought into stark relief the Nation's physical and economic vulnerability to attack within our borders. The relative ease with which terrorists were able to implement their plans serves as a pointed reminder to the Nation to identify critical 'soft spots' in the Nation's defenses. Among the Nation's vulnerabilities are our computer and communications networks, upon which the country's economic and critical infrastructures for finance, transportation, energy and water distribution, and health and emergency services depend.

The existence of these vulnerabilities has called into question the extent to which the Nation's research programs, educational system, and interconnected operations are able to meet the challenge of cyber warfare in the 21st century. Late last year, an editorial in *The Los Angeles Times* emphasized the importance of meeting this challenge: "A cyber terrorist attack would not carry the same shock and carnage of September 11. But in this information age. . .one could be more widespread and just as economically destructive."

However, the fact that our information networks are vulnerable to attack is not new. Several influential think tanks and government-sponsored blue-ribbon commissions—both civilian and military—outlined vulnerabilities U.S. information systems and made recommendations for more cyber security R&D. Such R&D would focus on broad areas including information assurance, intrusion monitoring and detection, vulnerability assessment and systems analysis, risk management decision support, mitigation, and incident response and recovery. These panels also called for the establishment of new partnerships between government, industry, and academia to ensure a focused R&D program.

The Science Committee held two hearings last year exploring the Nation's research and education capabilities in cyber security. More information can be found in the charters for first two Committee hearings on cyber security R&D:

— October 10, 2001 hearing entitled *Cyber Security—How Can We Protect American Computer Networks from Attack?*
http://www.house.gov/science/full/oct10/full_charter_101001.htm

— October 17, 2001 hearing entitled *Cyber Terrorism—A View From The Gilmore Commission,*
http://www.house.gov/science/full/oct17/full_charter_101701.htm

3. Defense Investments in Information Security

Much of the Nation's expertise in information security lies within the military and intelligence agencies. Secure transmission of information within the military has been a priority since the beginning of warfare. Over the years, military agencies inhouse military laboratories such as the Air Force Research Laboratory—Information Directorate at Rome, New York have developed tremendous R&D capabilities in information security. This capability is recognized by other defense and intelligence agencies such as the National Security Agency, Defense Advanced Research Projects Agency and others.

Unfortunately, defense investments in information security—especially basic and applied R&D—have not kept up with the increased demand for more secure and reliable military information systems. In March 2001, the Defense Science Board defined a slate of priorities for the Global Information Grid (GIG), a DOD information network system of "interconnected sensors and information systems," that uses DOD-unique software and system and commercial infrastructure. R&D, it said, was needed to develop new methods of "mobile code" to defend against attacks, and on forensics, tagging and trace back. It also called for "high leverage" R&D to maintain the Defense Information Infrastructure, including work on "scalable global access control, malicious code detection and mitigation, mobile code security, fault tolerance, integrity restoration, recovery and reconstitution." The Board recommended that R&D funding in these areas rise by $40 million in FY 2001 and $350 million over the next five years.

4. Greater Long-Term Civilian R&D Investments in Cyber Security Needed

At the same time defense investments in cyber security made by federal civilian R&D agencies such as the National Science Foundation were small or non-existent. This has led to a situation where the Nation's intellectual capacity in information security field has lagged behind the tremendous demand for greater security in major sectors of the U.S. economy.

The Science Committee held two hearings to examine how to best mobilize the Federal Government's science and technology enterprise to help protect American computer systems from attack. At those hearings experts including Dr. William Wulf, President of the National Academy of Engineering testified that with the possible exception of encryption related research, cyber security research has been chronically underfunded, and basic research into fundamental cyber security challenges is not robust enough to meet the Nation's needs. Simply put, when it comes to computer security, too few people are paying too little attention and coming up with too few ideas.

During the course of the hearings the Committee learned that cyber security has been a neglected field. Although numbers are difficult to come by, federally funded cyber security research may amount to less than $60 million per year. Experts believe that fewer than 100 U.S. researchers have the experience and expertise to conduct cutting edge research in cyber security. This is true even though a computer science department at a single research university may have 60 or more faculty members.

In response to testimony received at these hearings, the Science Committee reported out H.R. 3394, the Cyber Security Research and Development Act of 2002. H.R. 3394 passed the House by a vote of 400–12 and now awaits action in the Senate. H.R. 3394 is designed to address four inadequacies with current research efforts:

1. The Federal Government has chronically under-invested in cyber security, an area in which the private sector has little incentive to invest.
2. This is true, in part, because no Federal agency has the responsibility of ensuring that the Nation has a robust cyber security research enterprise;
3. As a result, what little research has been done on cyber security has been incremental, leaving the basic approaches to cyber security unchanged for decades; and
4. As a field with relatively little money, few researchers and minimal attention, cyber security fails to attract the interest of students, perpetuating the problems in the field.

5. Coordination of Federal Cyber Security Efforts

The Bush Administration has taken important steps to develop a capability to coordinate cyber security activities with the Nation's counter-terrorism effort. Information security R&D is an important component of these efforts. The mechanism established parallels with the organization created by the Clinton Administration.

In Executive Order 13231, October 16, 2001, the President created "The President's Critical Infrastructure Board," charged with preventing disruptions of critical infrastructure and information networks in water, telecommunication, financial and transportation, health care and emergency services and manufacturing. Although it is directed to work closely with industry and State and local governments, it is composed wholly of executive agency officials, including the OSTP Director and 24 other agency heads and officials. It is chaired by the Special Advisor to the President for

Cyberspace Security, who will report both to the Assistant for National Security and the Assistant for Homeland Security. The Board was given responsibility "to recommend policies and coordinate programs. . .." With respect to R&D, the board is mandated to:

> Coordinate with the Director of the Office of Science and Technology Policy (OSTP) on a program of Federal Government research and development for protection of information systems for critical infrastructure, including emergency preparedness communications, and the physical assets that support such systems, and ensure coordination of government activities in this field with corporations, universities, federally funded research centers, and national laboratories. In this function, the Board shall work in coordination with the National Science Foundation, the Defense Advanced Research Projects Agency, and with other departments and agencies, as appropriate.

The executive order established 10 standing committees, including one on Research and Development, chaired by a designee of the Director of OSTP. In addition to proposing plans for "subjects within its purview," and making recommendations to OMB on agency budgets "that fall within the Board's purview, after review of relevant program requirements and resources," the Board was given specific authority to "annually request the National Science Foundation, Department of Energy, Department of Transportation, Environmental Protection Agency, Department of Commerce, Departments of Defense, and the Intelligence Community. . .to include in their budget requests to OMB funding for demonstration projects and research to support the Board's activities."

On October 9, 2001, President Bush named Richard Clarke, the Clinton Administration Critical Infrastructure Coordinator, and considered to be an information security expert, to serve as his special advisor on cyber security and Director of the President's Critical Infrastructure Board. He was not specifically mentioned on the organizational chart as a member of the senior-level OHS Principals Committee, but he was listed among those who will attend meetings of the sub-Cabinet Deputies Committee if cyber security is discussed.

6. Improving Collaboration with Law Enforcement to Combat Cyber-Terrorism

In testimony before the Science Committee, Governor James Gilmore, Chairman of the National Advisory Panel to Assess Domestic Response Capabilities for Terrorism Involving Weapons of Mass Destruction (Gilmore Commission), noted that "cyber attacks incident" to conflicts in the Middle East "emphasized the potentially disastrous effects that such concentrated attacks can have on information and other critical government and private sector electronic systems." The Gilmore Commission concluded that while not "mass destructive," attacks on our critical infrastructure would certainly be "mass disruptive." It also concluded that the most likely perpetrators of cyber attacks on critical infrastructures are terrorists and criminal groups rather than nation-states. As a result, the Commission predicted that detection of these attacks would fall primarily to the private sector and to local law enforcement authorities.

In light of this, the Commission concluded that greater efforts must be made to establish effective partnerships with the private sector and to improve coordination with State and local governments. In particular, private sector cooperation is essential to response efforts in the areas of deterrence, detection, identification, prevention, response, recovery, and restoration.

Effective models of such cooperation have been developed, most notably in Central New York State. The National Law Enforcement and Corrections Technology Center—Northeast Region CyberScience Laboratory co-located at the Air Force Research Laboratory in Rome, New York is working with State, Federal and local law enforcement, as well as academia and the military on a daily basis in the fight against cyber terrorism. The CyberScience Laboratory has forged an effective partnership with the New York Electronic Crimes Task Force (see below) as well as the New York State Police and other law enforcement agencies to help catch criminals and terrorists who use the Internet and other electronic devices to perpetrate crimes.

On May 7, 2002 the House Judiciary Committee reported out H.R. 3482 the Cyber Security Enhancement Act of 2001—co-sponsored by Crime Subcommittee Lamar Smith and Science Committee Boehlert. H.R. 3482 would establish the creation of an Office of Science and Technology at the Department of Justice as well as explicitly authorize the National Law Enforcement Science and Technology Centers—expanding their visibility and paving the way for greater budget requests for activities such as the CyberScience Laboratory.

7. Department of Homeland Security

President Bush announced the creation of a Cabinet-level Department of Homeland Security on June 6, 2002. While details about the role of the Homeland Security Department remain unclear, protection of cyberspace will be a priority for the new agency. According to the Bush Administration, two existing entities with responsibility for protecting the U.S. cyber infrastructure from terrorist attack—the Critical Infrastructure Assurance Office (currently part of the Department of Commerce) and the National Infrastructure Protection Center (FBI)—will be merged into the new Homeland Security Department.

The Administration also proposes to merge the United States Secret Service (USSS) into the new department. The USSS has played an increasingly influential role in the war against terrorism through its expertise in tracking terrorist financial assets. In 1995, the Secret Service New York Field Office formed the New York Electronic Crimes Task Force with representatives from State, Federal and local law enforcement, prosecutors, academe, and experts from the business world. The Task Force was created to help counter criminal threats to U.S. information networks and to combat the growing criminal use of advanced technologies—particularly information technologies—including identity theft, credit card fraud and other information-age crimes.

The USA PATRIOT Act authorized the U.S. Secret Service to establish a nationwide network of Electronic Crimes Task Forces based upon the New York model. Task Forces have been expanded to major U.S. cities including: Boston, Charlotte, Chicago, Los Angeles, Miami, San Francisco, Washington, D.C., and Las Vegas.

8. Witnesses

Panel I

- — Hon. John H. Marburger, Ph.D., Science Advisor to the President & Director, White House Office of Science and Technology Policy
- — John S. Tritak, Director, White House Critical Infrastructure Assurance Office (CIAO)
- — Hon. James Engle, Ph.D., Deputy Undersecretary for Science and Technology, United States Air Force
- — James K. Kallstrom, Special Advisor for Public Security to Governor George S. Pataki

Panel II

- — Robert Weaver, Deputy Special Agent-in-Charge, New York Field Office; Director, New York Electronic Crimes Task Force, United States Secret Service
- — Dr. Yacov Shamash, Dean of Engineering, State University of New York at Stony Brook
- — Michael Miravalle, President & CEO, Dolphin Technologies, Inc., Rome, New York

9. Questions

1. What are the unmet challenges in computer/network security as they relate to terrorism? What types of research are needed to protect critical information systems from attack?
2. How can the Federal Government better leverage existing defense R&D capabilities in information assurance to counter cyber terrorist threats? Should the Federal Government expand technology transfer mechanisms—such as the National Institute of Justice CyberScience Laboratory at Rome, New York—to help Federal, State and local law enforcement and other homeland security agencies fight cyber terrorism?
3. How can government and/or federal funding help prioritize and encourage more industry and university-based research and cooperation in information assurance? How can research and education institutions in upstate New York—in particular the Air Force Research Laboratory-Information Directorate at Rome and New York's public and private colleges and universities—better collaborate and partner with industry in the information assurance field?
4. What are your views on current state of information assurance education and training? How can research and education institutions located in upstate New York better meet the growing demand for more individuals with backgrounds in information assurance and related fields?

Panel I

Dr. HUTTON. Good morning. Mr. Chairman, Members of the Committee and other distinguished guests. It's very nice to have you in Upstate New York.

As the President of Utica College, I would like to welcome everyone here this morning. The discussions that will take place here and the testimony that will be offered here today will undoubtedly yield significant results for the future. We are so honored to host this field hearing on homeland and cyber security as this is an issue of critical importance for our country and one that has been an area of focus for Utica College for many years.

The events of September 11, the subsequent acts of terrorism and the seemingly daily threats against our country have further emphasized the need to prepare professionals in the areas of preventing and detecting attacks on our nation's infrastructure.

Last month, we graduated our second class of students from our Economic Crime Management Master's Program. This graduating class featured top executives from private industries as well as representatives from key law enforcement and government agencies. This group also included students who had just a few years earlier completed their undergraduate studies in economic crime investigation at Utica College.

I mention this because many years ago Utica College anticipated the dire shortage of professionals possessing an understanding of economic crime and the ability to combat this emerging, complex crime wave. In fact, Utica College was the first institution in the world to launch a graduate level program devoted exclusively to the prevention and detection of economic crime.

I applaud the efforts of our legislators in this room and in Washington who have worked diligently to bring a global focus to this urgent issue, and Utica College is proud to partner in these efforts.

Once again, in closing, I would like to welcome everyone here this morning. All of us in this auditorium today are deeply committed to strengthening our country's defense against computer-related crime. I am confident that this field hearing at Utica College will go a long way in helping us achieve that goal.

Once again, welcome to Upstate New York.

[Applause.]

Chairman BOEHLERT. The hearing will come to order.

Thank you very much, Dr. Hutton.

I'm going to deviate from the normal practice and start this hearing with a pledge to the flag. Because there is special significance not only in the subject matter we are dealing with here today, cyber security and homeland defense, but the very fact that behind me is the flag that flew over 7 World Trade Center, brought here by Special Agent Bob Weaver of the Secret Service. It has special meaning as does this very important hearing that we're having today.

By virtue of the caliber of the witnesses, I want all of you to know this is very serious business, and we are so pleased to bring this hearing to this campus in this city and this state at this very poignant time.

Would you join me now in pledging the flag.

[Whereupon, the assemblage joined in the Pledge of Allegiance to the Flag.]

Chairman BOEHLERT. Thank you so very much. I want to welcome everyone here today for this hearing. I greatly appreciate my colleagues joining me here, and I want especially to offer my thanks to the top officials from the Federal and State Government who have taken time to join us here today.

You will have the opportunity to hear this morning from some of the leading figures in our government's effort to protect our nation from terrorists, starting with the President's Science Advisor, Dr. John Marburger—a long-time New Yorker, I might add. And just as importantly, these leaders from Washington will have a chance to learn how much our area can contribute to the war on terrorism, both from the testimony they will hear and from a tour we will take later of the Air Force Research Laboratory in Rome.

Indeed, the purpose of this hearing is to learn more about the risks of Upstate New York and what we face, how Federal programs can help us address those risks and how our area can contribute to and benefit from these Federal programs. So there's plenty to discuss.

The risks we're going to focus on most today concern cyber security. Now, the average Central New Yorker might, understandably, believe that they have nothing to fear from a cyber attack, but unfortunately, that's simply not the case. In our evermore networked world, we have all had an incredible stake and we continue to have that stake in keeping our computer systems up and running. Our nation's defenses, our financial systems, our utilities, our communications systems, all rely on computer networks to operate. This is not something of concern to just a few, isolated computer geeks. It's something that must concern us all.

Yet, until recently, only a relatively few were concerned with this problem. The Science Committee has learned from our previous hearings on this subject that the Federal Government, industry and academia have all tended to downplay computer security as an area of necessary research.

As a result, too few top researchers have worked in this field, too few students have been attracted to it, and too few innovative solutions have been developed to protect our computers and networks.

Cyber security is clearly an area where the safety of our country depends on getting more and better research done, and done fast.

That's why I was so pleased when the first hearing, early after the new session, the Science Committee passed and then, subsequently, the full house passed our bill, the "Cyber Security Research and Development Act," to create new programs to ensure that there is a focused effort to improve computer security.

It is also one reason why I was so pleased when the President announced his proposal to create a new Department of Homeland Security, one portion of which will be dedicated to cyber security and other infrastructure protection. The Science Committee is reviewing the proposal now, and we will have a very key role to play as this unfolds and evolves into meaningful legislation. I'm so glad to have so many people here from so many different important sources of information, and we look forward to the testimony.

I ask unanimous consent that the remainder of my statement be enclosed in the record in its entirety for future reference.

The Chair will now recognizes Mrs. Lee from the great State of Texas.

[The prepared statement of Chairman Boehlert follows:]

PREPARED STATEMENT OF CHAIRMAN SHERWOOD BOEHLERT

I want to welcome everyone here today for this important hearing. I greatly appreciate my colleagues joining me here, and I want especially to offer my thanks to the top federal officials who have taken the time to join us today.

We will have the opportunity to hear this morning from some of the leading figures in our government's effort to protect our nation from terrorists, starting with the President's Science Advisor, Dr. Marburger—a longtime New Yorker, I should note. And just as importantly, these leaders from Washington will have a chance to learn how much our area can contribute to the war on terrorism—both from the testimony they will hear today and from the tour we will take later of the Air Force laboratory in Rome.

Indeed, the purpose of this hearing is to learn more about the risks upstate New York faces, how federal programs can help us address those risks, and how our area can contribute to, and benefit from those federal programs. So, there's plenty to discuss.

The risks we're going to focus on most today concern cyber security. Now, the average Utican might, understandably, believe that they have nothing to fear from a cyber attack, but unfortunately, that's not the case. In our ever more networked world, we all have an incredible stake in keeping our computer systems up and running. Our nation's defenses, our financial system, our local utilities, our communications systems all rely on computer networks to operate. This is not something of concern to just a few, isolated computer geeks.

Yet, until recently, only a relatively few, isolated people were concerned with this problem. The Science Committee has learned from our previous hearings on this subject, that the Federal Government, industry and academia all have tended to downplay computer security as an area of research.

As a result, too few top researchers have worked in this field, too few students have been attracted to it, and too few innovative solutions have been developed to protect our computers and networks. Cyber security is clearly an area where the safety of our country depends on getting more and better research done—and done fast.

That's why I was so pleased when first the Science Committee and then the House passed my bill, "the Cyber Security Research and Development Act," to create new programs to ensure that there is a focused federal effort to improve computer security.

It's also one reason I was so pleased when the President announced his proposal to create a Department of Homeland Security, one portion of which will be dedicated to cyber security and other infrastructure protection. The Science Committee is reviewing the proposal now, and we will approve it with whatever modifications we decide are needed by July 12.

The testimony we receive today will help us sort through the issues raised by the President's proposal. We also will hold Science Committee hearings in Washington both tomorrow and Thursday to learn more about the Department of Homeland Security. Tomorrow we'll be hearing from the National Academy of Sciences about a new report on how research and development can contribute to homeland security.

The heightened focus on homeland security in general, and cyber security, in particular, should bring additional attention to some of the resources our own area can bring to this work. In addition to our great university research centers, we have Rome Laboratory, with its very relevant focus on C4I work, and the National Institute of Justice Center at Rome.

The NIJ Center has been directly involved in efforts to combat computer crime terrorists are not the only threat to cyber security—having provided their expertise and assistance to the New York Electronic Crimes Task Force. This Task Force, led by the New York office of the Secret Service, is a model of crime-fighting that is now being replicated in other cities. And, interestingly, the Secret Service is one of the agencies that the President proposes to move into the Department of Homeland Security.

Sadly, the Task Force has had to bear the brunt of terrorism quite directly. Their offices were in 7 World Trade Center, which collapsed on September 11. Happily, everyone got out of that building safely. One of our witnesses, Special Agent Bob

Weaver, has brought us today the flag that flew over 7 World Trade Center. This is a very stark and moving reminder of why the topic we will be discussing today is so important. I thank Bob for all his work and for sharing the flag with us today.

We will need to be sure that the capabilities of Bob's team can only expand in the years ahead.

So, I look forward to hearing from today's witnesses what we need to do today to ensure that we have the protections we need tomorrow. And I look forward to showing off how our area can help do whatever needs to be done. Let's begin.

Ms. JACKSON LEE. Thank you very much, Mr. Chairman.

It's a pleasure to be with you here at Utica College and to all of those who are joining us for this very important hearing.

Might I, too, express my appreciation to the Chairman for his leadership, recognizing the enormous tragedy reflected by this flag that this nation experienced. I was very proud to be part of the Science Committee that immediately took action to assess parts of the issues that were under its jurisdiction.

The legislation that was passed, the "Cyber Security Research and Development Act," was to help create a more critical mass of individuals trained to be able to address the question of cyber security.

Let me say that I believe we can do it, and I believe that because we did do it premillennium—when we were very much concerned about the impact that the millennium would have on our cyber and security systems. We handled it then. I believe we can handle it now.

We know after the tragic events of September 11, it goes without saying that national security is foremost in everyone's mind. As we work to improve our country's security, it is important that we take inventory of all systems that are vital to the functioning of the Nation and do all we can to protect them.

I am delighted to be here and to be here as a senior member of the Science Committee and to bring the respective greetings of the Ranking Member, Mr. Ralph Hall.

This certainly includes our computer network systems that can be attacked anonymously and from far away. These networks are the glue that holds our nation's infrastructure together. An attack from cyberspace could jeopardize electric power grids, railways, hospitals and financial services, to name a few.

Coming from Texas with the Texas Medical Center, we've seen firsthand the enormous impact when the medical center is not functioning, and so it is important that we begin to look at sources to protect these valuable assets of the United States.

We are all aware of the growing number of Internet security incidences, involving such things as computer viruses, denial of service attacks and defaced websites. These events have disrupted business and government activities and have sometimes resulted in recovery costs.

As a member of the House Judiciary Committee, I would like to ask that we are certainly aware of the need for providing the communication system, transfer of information, talking to each other, and that should be part of what we think of as we look at protecting our cyberspace security needs.

While we have been fortunate so far in avoiding a catastrophic cyber attack, Richard Clarke, the President's cyber terrorism czar, has said that the government must make cyber security a priority or face the possibility of a "digital Pearl Harbor."

In the Committee's previous hearings on this topic last fall, we learned that the Nation has been underinvesting in information security R&D. One result of anemic funding has been an inability to move beyond near term, incremental research. It is time for a broad-reaching, forward-thinking approach. That is what our enemy will do, and we must be one step ahead of them.

We also found that too few scientists and engineers are working on problems in information security. I am delighted to be here to take note, Mr. President, of the economic, if you will, crime program that you have here at Utica College. Very timely, and we're delighted at that program.

The future of the industry is further endangered by the lack of resources, which has discouraged talented young computer scientists and engineers from entering the field.

I'm very glad that the Chairman has that as part of his agenda for the Science Committee to provide the opportunity for more to be trained in research and development in these areas.

Furthermore, the people that do work on information security are scattered through industry, academia and government. Our past witnesses have suggested the need for better coordination of R&D activities among these groups. This still needs to be addressed. As we move toward developing a Homeland Security Department, as it is being created, let us find a viable place for cyberspace security and let us find an opportunity for these matters to have oversight by the Science Committee.

This morning, we look forward to the recommendations and advice of our witnesses. I will be interested in any thoughts our panelists may have on how to develop the human resource base of research scientists and computer security professionals that the country will need.

As I started out by saying, Mr. Chairman, I welcome these witnesses. I believe that the leadership they provide will be particularly insightful, and I do believe we have the insight to ensure that we protect our nation, our homeland and provide the insight and the talent that would help you to do this.

I ask unanimous consent that my statement in its entirety be submitted in the records of this committee.

[The prepared statement of Ms. Lee follows:]

PREPARED STATEMENT OF REPRESENTATIVE SHEILA JACKSON LEE

Mr. Chairman, I am pleased to join you here today at Utica College for this important hearing on the security of cyberspace.

After the tragic events of September 11th, it goes without saying that national security is foremost in everyone's mind. As we work to improve our country's security, it is important that we take inventory of all systems that are vital to the functioning of the Nation, and do all we can to protect them.

This certainly includes our computer networks systems that can be attacked anonymously and from far away. These networks are the glue that holds our nation's infrastructure together. An attack from cyberspace could jeopardize electric power grids, railways, hospitals and financial services, to name a few.

We are all aware of the growing number of Internet security incidents, involving such things as computer viruses, denial of service attacks, and defaced web sites. These events have disrupted business and government activities, and have sometimes resulted in significant recovery costs.

While we have been fortunate so far in avoiding a catastrophic cyber attack, Richard Clarke, the President's cyber terrorism czar, has said that the government must make cyber security a priority or face the possibility of a "Digital Pearl Harbor."

In the Committee's previous hearings on this topic last fall, we learned that the Nation has been under-investing in information security R&D. One result of anemic funding has been an inability to move beyond near-term, incremental research.

It is time for a broad-reaching, forward-thinking approach. That is what our enemy will do, and we must be one step ahead.

We also found that too few scientists and engineers are working on problems in information security. The future of the industry is further endangered by the lack of resources, which has discouraged talented young computer scientists and engineers from entering the field.

Furthermore, the people that do work on information security are scattered through industry, academia, and government. Our past witnesses have suggested the need for better coordination of R&D activities among these groups. This still needs to be addressed.

At present there is no home within the Federal Government for support of information security research. Long-term research is especially lacking. We need to ensure this critical problem is resolved.

This morning, we look forward to the advice and recommendations of our distinguished witnesses, especially as they relate to specific research needs, and to policy oversight and coordination of federal research on networked information systems.

I am also very interested in any thoughts our panelists may have on how to develop the human resource base of research scientists and computer security professionals that the country needs.

Finally, I would welcome our panelists comments and suggestions on how to ensure that new discoveries coming from research find their way into security products and applications.

I would like to thank Chairman Boehlert for organizing this important hearing. I appreciate the attendance of our witnesses, and I look forward to a productive discussion.

Chairman BOEHLERT. Without objection, so ordered. The Chair recognizes Mr. Smith of Michigan. Mr. Smith is the distinguished Chairman of the Subcommittee on Research.

Mr. Smith.

Mr. SMITH. Mr. Chairman, first let me thank you for holding the third in a series of these hearings. The Science Committee has a lot of activities, is responsible for a lot of the science activity that takes place in the United States government. Our chairman actually wrote and introduced the Cyber Security Research Development Act, that's 3394 that he earlier mentioned.

I have introduced—it's out of committee, and I think it's also important, Mr. Chairman, that we move ahead with the Information Technology Bill, 3400. I hope we can do that in the near future.

Government has been somewhat lax in our effort to do appropriate research and development to assure greater protection against cyber security. We are a nation that's become more and more dependent on computers and software, whether it's the running of a college or university, tracking people, our data bases, the way we generate and transmit electricity, the way we travel. So a great potential for disruption.

I just would like to offer my personal opinion, though, that while government has not done as much as it should, the private sector also needs to be more actively involved in the development of the kind of protections that are going to protect their particular industries. So my encouragement would be to the private sector not to just depend on what government does but to be active in your own areas of responsibility, in your own industries to help protect your particular industry.

And thank you, Mr. Chairman.

[The prepared statement of Mr. Smith follows:]

PREPARED STATEMENT OF REPRESENTATIVE NICK SMITH

Cyber Terrorism—Are We Prepared for the Next Attack?

I would like to thank Chairman Boehlert for holding this field hearing today on a matter of the utmost importance to this nation, cyber terrorism. As we all know, last September's attacks brought into sharp focus how vulnerable we are to attacks of terrorism: We responded to these challenges with an effective, sustained war effort abroad, but we also face new threats to our safety and security here on our own soil. The President has responded with a proposal that would make sweeping changes to the structure of our Federal Government. I believe that this proposal is a positive step that is not only warranted, but is necessary.

A critical component of the new Department's efforts in securing the Homeland will be to defend our vast networks of computer infrastructure. The threats to this infrastructure are real, substantial, and present challenges unprecedented in warfare. The level of sophistication and integration of computer systems into not only our military operations, but also our daily activities, while improving our lives substantially, have also increased our dependence on these systems. The result is the creation of targets that never before existed—targets of interconnected networks that are relied upon by millions of Americans and span the entire geographic area of the country. Physical security is now indelibly tied to cyber security. The potential damage by a successful attack on these systems is almost incomprehensible.

Immediately after the attacks, the Science Committee held hearings examining our vulnerability to cyber attacks in detail. From these hearings, Chairman Boehlert led the Committee in developing H.R. 3394, the Cyber-Security Research and Development Act. This bill establishes a research plan among several agencies to secure our nation's computer systems. It has passed the House and a similar version is moving ahead in the Senate. In addition to cyber security, the Committee has reported out legislation that I introduced, H.R. 3400, which updates and reauthorizes federal support for basic research in information technology. These investments will not only help us defend ourselves from cyber attacks of all kinds, but will help us to develop the tools we need for continued growth in our economy while we fight what is expected to be a long, difficult war.

There is, of course, more we can do, most notably with regard to ensuring that cyber security issues are appropriately addressed as we formulate the Department of Homeland Security. We have an excellent panel of witnesses here today and I am eager to hear their thoughts on these important issues.

Chairman BOEHLERT. Thank you very much.

The Chair recognizes the distinguished gentleman from Maryland, Dr. Roscoe Bartlett, Chairman of the Subcommittee on Energy.

Dr. Bartlett.

Mr. BARTLETT. Thank you.

Mr. Chairman, in our society there are two features which, in their aggregate, are clearly a zero sum gain: openness and security.

It's very clear that the more you have of one, the less you are going to have of another. And before September, but less than 10 months ago now, we had enormous openness and very little security. America is now trying to decide where along that continuum between total openness and total security we as a society need to come to rest.

And as a subset of that dialogue, we also need to address how much investment we're willing to make in security, and this is a very important hearing. Thank you for calling it, sir.

This is a very important hearing that continues the dialogue that will help us to determine how much of our openness we're willing to give up, at what cost, so that we can have additional security.

Thank you.

Chairman BOEHLERT. Thank you very much, Dr. Bartlett, and I want to thank all of my colleagues. You should know that Congress on occasion takes its show on the road, if you will, and conducts field hearings at strategic locations around the country. It is important for us to get out of Washington into the heartland of America and it's important for the heartland of America to be exposed to Congress and congressional hearings.

Of necessity, we limit the size and scope of these. But this is particularly significant, and that's why I'm so pleased that Mrs. Jackson Lee, Senior Democrat, and two subcommittee chairmen are here with me, which indicates the importance of this hearing. And when you consider the distinguished panel that you have, you begin to appreciate the dimensions and importance of this issue.

Now, I am pleased to announce our panel. The first panel consists of Dr. John H. Marburger, Science Advisor to the President of the United States and Director of the White House Office of Science and Technology Policy.

Mr. James K. Kallstrom, Special Advisor to the Governor, New York State Office of Public Security.

And it's good to see you back. You were an expert witness for us in Washington. It's nice to have you as a witness here on the home front.

Incidentally, Dr. Marburger is a New Yorker. I want to remind all of you of that.

Mr. John S. Tritak, Director, the White House Critical Infrastructure Assurance Office.

And Dr. James Engle, Deputy Undersecretary for Science and Technology, United States Air Force.

Gentlemen, we will expect an opening statement of approximately five minutes. We won't be arbitrary, but we prefer that you keep it to approximately that, which allows more time for questioning; and, obviously, your entire statement will appear in the record at this juncture.

Dr. Marburger, we start off with you.

STATEMENT OF DR. JOHN H. MARBURGER, SCIENCE ADVISOR TO THE PRESIDENT; DIRECTOR, WHITE HOUSE OFFICE OF SCIENCE AND TECHNOLOGY POLICY, WASHINGTON, D.C.

Dr. MARBURGER. Thank you, Mr. Chairman and Members of the Committee, and thank you for the opportunity to speak to you today about the efforts of the Office of Science and Technology Policy in the area of critical infrastructure protection, research and development.

Your committee has provided leadership in the Congress on this issue, and the administration looks forward to continuing to work with you to ensure that our critical systems are protected.

President Bush signaled his support for critical infrastructure protection efforts by issuing Executive Order 13231, entitled "Critical Infrastructure Protection In The Information Age."

This Order established the President's Critical Infrastructure Protection Board and several standing committees. Richard Clarke, Special Advisor to the President for cyberspace security, chairs the Board, and I chair the standing Committee for Research and Development. I'm going to refer to that as CR&D. I have included a chart in the last page of my testimony which sketches out the relationship of the various organizations and I will focus my remarks on the work of the CR&D which I chair.

It's a rather complicated committee. It covers a lot. It is expected that we would have a rather complicated structure to cover all of the issues that are involved, so I will have to make my oral remarks incomplete and refer you to the complete testimony for all of the examples and so forth.

The CR&D is tasked with coordinating a program of Federal Government research and development for the protection of information systems for critical infrastructure, including emergency preparedness, communications, and the physical assets that support these systems. In addition, the CR&D is tasked with ensuring coordination of government activities—and there are many of them—in this field with corporations, universities, federally funded research centers, and national laboratories.

Our vision is that of an United States whose critical infrastructures are trustworthy and resilient; that is, that they are able to provide a level of performance expected under a variety of conditions. They should have the ability to absorb intentional or unintentional outages with minimal impact on their ability to deliver needed levels of service, both directly to consumers and to the other infrastructures that depend on them.

Now, this challenge would prove daunting even if the technology of these critical infrastructures was static, but it's not. As we know, the technology embedded throughout the U.S. Economy is undergoing a continuous and profound transformation. Accordingly, our committee has sought to support the development of technologies that will counter threats and reduce vulnerabilities in those areas having potential for causing significant national security, economic and social impacts.

The overall objective of the Federal program in critical infrastructure protection R&D is to promote and to coordinate research to reduce vulnerabilities in our nation's critical infrastructure, and to promote the research and development of technologies that will detect, contain and mitigate attacks against failures in these infrastructures.

Now, I will give some specific examples. But before I do, I would like to say a few words about the budget and the funds that are allocated to this.

The Federal R&D budget is a very important tool for accomplishing national objectives, as you know, in critical infrastructure protection, Mr. Chairman.

The President's proposed budget for 2002–2003 calls for total Federal spending of $2.1 trillion. Of that amount, $3.9 billion is for critical infrastructure protection, quite a significant amount. The R&D portion of critical infrastructure protection budget is estimated to be about $870 million—$869.83 it says here, which is not insignificant.

The President has requested these funds on behalf of the agencies, and there are many of them, that will carry out the R&D programs that address the needs of the critical infrastructure protection effort.

So now let me describe the committee.

The critical infrastructure panel's CR&D Committee executes its coordinating function through eight working groups including: Information and communication, banking and finance, energy, transportation, vital human services, interdependencies, outreach and physical asset protection.

The first five sectors which were drawn from the 1997 Marsh Commission report on critical infrastructure protection, critical foundations. Following the example of the Marsh report, our committee merged emergency services, government services and water supply systems into the "vital human services" category and electrical power, oil, natural gas production and storage into the "energy" category.

The CR&D established subgroups corresponding to each of these sectors as well as a separate subgroup to address interdependencies among these sectors. It further established special subgroups to address outreach and physical asset protection issues.

Attachment A of my prepared remarks illustrates how this committee relates to the Office of Homeland Security and the National Security Council and the President's National Science and Technology Council.

Now, the reason I'm going through this is to indicate the great efforts that we've made to cover all of the areas that are affected by these critical infrastructures. There are many agencies involved in many issues, and we made an effort to be systematic in our coverage of them. It's a rather complicated structure, but we're organized. We meet regularly and try to stay on top of it.

These critical infrastructures that I mentioned are highly interdependent, both physically and in their greater reliance on the national information infrastructure. This trend has been accelerating in recent years with the explosive growth of information technology and shows no sign of abating. Potential threats to the normal functioning of these infrastructures are both natural and man-made. Individual outages can still prove serious, but this growing degree of interdependence can make possible a whole new scale of synergistic, non-linear consequences.

The responsibility for R&D issues in the President's Critical Infrastructure Protection Board as well as the Office of Homeland Security both reside in OSTP, my office, where there is a high level of coordination on such matters. Indeed, a joint working group on protection of physical infrastructures has been established to merge the efforts of the physical asset protection working group under the Critical Infrastructure Committee for R&D and the protection of vulnerable systems working group under the National Science and Technology Council Anti-Terrorism Task Force.

There's a lot of interconnection among the groups that are concerned with these issues.

I'm going to try to keep my remarks brief. There are a number of examples in my submitted testimony of the activities of each one of these panels, so that you can get a concrete idea of the nature of their work from those. And I will be glad to respond to questions.

But before I conclude my remarks, I would like to make an important point, which is that the education of the next generation of researchers and professors in information assurance and security technology is of critical national importance. The Administration has made inroads in this area by introducing scholarship funding into universities across America. The Cyber Corps Scholarships for Services Program encourages college students to become high tech computer security professionals within the government. Managed by the National Science Foundation and the Office of Personnel Management, this program also helps build academic programs at universities in the area of computer security.

There are many more examples of activities that are included in my written statement. But before I conclude, I do want to commend the Chairman and Members of this committee for their efforts to strengthen our critical infrastructure systems. Legislation such as H.R. 3394, the Cyber Security R&D Act, goes a long way in addressing requirements for computer network security research, and we look forward to continuing to work with you and other Members of Congress on the right funding levels and priorities for these programs.

Mr. Chairman, at this point, I will be pleased to answer questions.

Chairman BOEHLERT. Thank you very much, Dr. Marburger.

[The prepared statement of Dr. Marburger follows:]

PREPARED STATEMENT OF JOHN H. MARBURGER

Mr. Chairman and Members of the Committee, thank you for the opportunity to speak to you today about the efforts of the Office of Science and Technology Policy (OSTP) in the area of critical infrastructure protection (CIP) research and development.

President Bush signaled his support for critical infrastructure protection efforts by issuing Executive Order 13231 (E.O. 13231), "Critical Infrastructure Protection in the Information Age." E.O. 13231, signed October 16, 2001, stated that it is U.S. policy "to protect against the disruption of the operation of information systems for critical infrastructure. . .and to ensure that any disruptions that occur are infrequent, of minimal duration, and manageable, and cause the least damage possible." This Order established the President's Critical Infrastructure Protection Board and several standing committees. Richard Clarke, Special Advisor to the President for Cyberspace Security, chairs the Board, and I chair the Standing Committee for Research and Development (CR&D).

The CR&D is tasked with coordinating a program of Federal Government research and development for protection of information systems for critical infrastructure, including emergency preparedness communications and the physical assets that support such systems. In addition, the CR&D is tasked with ensuring coordination of government activities in this field with corporations, universities, federally funded research centers, and national laboratories.

As you know, President Bush recently unveiled the plan to create a Department of Homeland Security. His decision to take this monumental step—the most sweeping reorganization of our national security establishment in over 50 years—was made on the basis of careful study and experience gained since September 11. The new Department of Homeland Security would be organized into four divisions: Border and Transportation Security; Emergency Preparedness and Response; Chemical, Biological, Radiological and Nuclear Countermeasures; and Information Analysis and Infrastructure Protection. CIP R&D will be a component of the Department's efforts, and the CR&D will coordinate the research efforts of this and other agencies.

VISION

The vision to which the CR&D has focused its efforts is that of a United States whose critical infrastructures are trustworthy and resilient. That is, they are able to provide the level of performance expected under a variety of conditions. To achieve this goal, they should have the ability to absorb intentional or unintentional outages with minimal impact on their ability to deliver needed levels of service, both to consumers directly and to the other infrastructures that depend upon them. This challenge would prove daunting even if the technologies of these critical infrastructures were static. As we know, the technology embedded throughout the U.S. economy is undergoing a continuous and profound transformation. Accordingly, the CR&D has sought to support the development of technologies that will counter threats and reduce vulnerabilities in those areas having potential for causing significant national security, economic, and social impacts.

Such a robust set of critical infrastructures would have assured continuity, viability, and protection from hostile acts and natural outages that would significantly diminish the abilities of the Federal Government to perform essential national security missions. This robustness must also be extended to: ensure the general public health and safety; permit state and local governments to maintain order and deliver essential public services; and allow the private sector to continue the orderly functioning of the economy and the delivery of essential information and communications, energy, financial, transportation, and other services.

As part of the vision, any interruption or manipulation of these critical functions would be brief, predictable in impact, infrequent, manageable, geographically isolated, and minimally detrimental to the welfare of the United States.

To help realize this vision, our goal is to identify and to support a vigorous and effective program of federal R&D in critical infrastructure protection. This program, along with private sector efforts, should enhance the security of our nation's critical infrastructures by rapidly identifying, developing, and facilitating the fielding of technological solutions, management tools, and techniques to address existing and emerging infrastructure threats and vulnerabilities.

The overall objective of the federal program in critical infrastructure protection R&D is to promote and coordinate research to reduce vulnerabilities in our nation's critical infrastructure, and to support the research and development of technologies that will detect, contain, and mitigate attacks against or other failures in these infrastructures.

BUDGET

The federal research and development budget is an important tool for accomplishing national objectives in critical infrastructure protection.

- The President's proposed budget for 2003 calls for total federal spending of $2.1 trillion.
- Of that amount, $3.9 billion is for critical infrastructure protection.
- The R&D portion of critical infrastructure protection budget is estimated to be $870 million.

The President has requested these funds on behalf of the agencies that will carry out the R&D programs that address the needs of the critical infrastructure protection effort.

OPERATIONALIZING THE VISION AND LONG-TERM GOAL

The CIP CR&D executes its coordinating function through eight working groups including:

- Information and Communication
- Banking and Finance
- Energy
- Transportation
- Vital Human Services (including water, emergency services, government services/defense)
- Interdependencies
- Outreach
- Physical Asset Protection

The first five sectors were drawn by the 1997 Marsh Commission report on Critical Infrastructure Protection, Critical Foundations. As that report did, the CR&D merged Emergency Services, Government Services, and Water Supply Systems into the Vital Human Services category, and Electrical Power and Oil and Natural Gas Production and Storage into the Energy category. The CR&D established subgroups that correspond to each of these sectors, as well as a separate subgroup to address interdependencies among these sectors. It further established special subgroups to address outreach and physical asset protection issues.

The above critical infrastructures are highly interdependent, both physically and in their greater reliance on the national information infrastructure. This trend has been accelerating in recent years with the explosive growth of information technology (IT) and shows no sign of abating. Potential threats to the normal functioning of these infrastructures are both natural and man-made. Individual outages can still prove serious, but this growing degree of interconnectedness can make possible a whole new scale of synergistic, nonlinear consequences.

The responsibility for R&D issues in the President's Critical Infrastructure Protection Board as well as the Office of Homeland Security both reside in OSTP, as there is a high level of coordination on such matters. Indeed, a joint working group on protection of physical infrastructures has been established to merge the efforts of the Physical Asset Protection Working Group under the CIP Committee for R&D and the Protection of Vulnerable Systems Working Group under the National Science and Technology Council (NSTC) Anti-Terrorism Task Force.

OSTP also maintains regular contact with numerous science, engineering, and technology societies, as well as higher education organizations.

SECTOR R&D

OSTP has adopted a straightforward approach to developing a Federal Government CIP R&D agenda. After preliminary briefings on the nature of the problem, the CR&D working groups identify the major vulnerabilities of each sector, as well as the existing CIP R&D work and programs already funded by the Federal Government in each sector. The working groups then sketch out an ideal, fiscally unconstrained set of programs to address the vulnerabilities in each sector. The gaps between the ideal and what is currently being undertaken then form the raw material from which to develop an R&D agenda for a current fiscal year and beyond. This year's objectives, challenges and major efforts underway are detailed in OSTP's submission for the National Plan for Cyber Security. The following are excerpts from OSTP's submission.

Information and Communications Sector (I&C). For FY 2002, 15 federal departments or agencies requested funds in the President's budget submitted to Congress for 87 ongoing I&C CIP R&D programs. The research areas or topics these programs address run the gamut from public key infrastructure and Internet security to mobile agents and advanced authentication systems.

Many of these programs are cooperative endeavors or joint efforts among different departments, and a few are joint efforts between government and academia. The Department of Defense's "Critical Infrastructure Protection and High Confidence, Adaptable Software University Research Initiative" is an example of expanded research opportunities across a range of selected topics deemed crucial to our CIP needs. The Department of Defense (DOD) plays a major role in addressing CIP issues across the spectrum of R&D efforts. Active CIP R&D programs are present throughout DOD, and they continue to receive strong congressional support.

Focus areas for the I&C sector include:

- Threat/Vulnerability/Risk Assessments—focusing on threat, vulnerability, and risk assessments of the I&C critical infrastructure to include modeling and simulation programs, metrics, and testbeds;
- System Protection—focusing on cyber protection of individual systems, to include programs such as encryption, public key infrastructures, network security products, reliability and security of computing systems, robust I&C control systems, and secure supervisory control and data acquisition (SCADA) systems;
- Intrusion Monitoring and Response—focusing on technologies to detect and to provide immediate responses to intrusions or infrastructure attacks to include such programs as network intrusion detection, information assurance technologies, mobile code and agents, network alarm systems, forensic tools for electronic media, and network defensive technologies; and
- Recovery and Reconstitution—focusing on those technologies required to reconstitute and restore the I&C critical infrastructure in the aftermath of disruptions to include such programs as risk management studies and tools, system survivability technologies, and consequence analysis tools and supporting technologies.

Banking and Finance Sector. While the Banking and Finance sector critical infrastructure has some unique elements, it primarily consists of important subsets of the other infrastructures, especially the Information and Communications infrastructure. While some vulnerabilities and threats are unique to the Banking and Finance sector, the greatest part of the sector's risk is inherited from the underlying supporting infrastructures.

A complicating factor in coordinating R&D in the Banking and Finance sector is that there has been little R&D of any kind done in this community. The only work that fits a traditional definition of R&D is the development of new derivatives and financial forecasting tools. Consequently, this area has no tradition of R&D. In addition, it lacks the research personnel in the community necessary to oversee the required work.

To address the new and expanding threats from foreign nation states, criminal enterprises and terrorists, the community has sponsored a number of initiatives with the support of the Treasury Department. In addition to the Information Sharing and Vulnerability Assessment Center, a research and development working group with private industry leadership exists. This working group has identified what research is being done within the community and has vetted the efforts underway within the government and Information and Communications sector. The working group also supports the protection of the Banking and Finance sector critical infrastructure. The Banking Information Technology Group under the Bankers Roundtable is also examining requirements in this area.

One major result of this review is the initiation of a modeling project, scheduled to begin in the later part of FY 2002. This project will identify the vulnerabilities in the Banking and Finance sector critical infrastructure. It will build on work of the National Coordinating Center for Telecommunications under the Office the Manager National Communications System, which has completed an extensive model of the U.S. backbone communications network. This object-oriented model is aimed at understanding the properties, vulnerabilities, and required remediation for our national communications infrastructure.

Energy Sector. Our nation's energy infrastructure—composed of increasingly interdependent industries that produce and distribute electric power, oil, and natural gas—is undergoing rapid and dramatic changes. Advances in information technology, an increased reliance on electronic commerce, restructuring and deregulation initiatives, and other market forces are motivating much of these changes. Applicable R&D encompasses both the physical and cyber components of the electric power, oil, and gas infrastructures, the interdependencies among those components, and the interdependencies with the other critical national infrastructures.

The R&D agenda consists of two primary thrust areas:

- Analysis and Risk Management, and
- Protection and Mitigation Technologies

Examples of research within the thrust areas include:

- Vulnerability Assessments. Researchers are continuing to expand collaborative efforts with the national energy sector to conduct physical and cyber vulnerability assessments.
- Infrastructure Interdependencies. Researchers are developing methodologies and tools for characterizing and analyzing interdependencies among the energy infrastructures and with other critical infrastructures. This capability will help the Department of Energy (DOE) and others within the energy sector identify critical system nodes and assess the technical, economic, and national security implications of energy technology and policy decisions designed to ensure the security of our nation's interdependent energy systems.
- High Security Supervisory Control and Data Acquisition (SCADA) Systems. Work has begun to develop next-generation security technologies (hardware and software) for the real-time process control, supervisory, and data collection systems (SCADA and Energy Management and Control Systems) now central to the functionality and integrity of the energy generation and distribution infrastructure.
- Flexible Automation Technology and Encryption Standards. A requirement exists to develop technologies to provide real-time encryption, identification and authentication, and continuous monitoring to prevent and detect intrusion. We must also develop standards for robust security for all energy infrastructure systems and networks.
- Sensor and Warning Technology. Improvement of existing integrated systems or development of new systems to warn of attacks and impending failures at critical nodes. We must focus on anomaly detection and failure warning technologies.
- Transmission and Distribution—Electricity. This area includes research on national-level grid monitoring and detection as well as electric system vulnerability assessments tools.
- Analysis of Scale, Complexity of Energy Systems. Research on the fundamental operational characteristics of large-scale, complex, non-linear energy infrastructures. Develop technologies and capabilities that focus on stability, countermeasures, reduction of complexity, the effects of uncertainty, and be-

havior. Development of databases, analytic tools and visualization techniques in order to assure the safe and reliable operation of the infrastructure.

The R&D areas that DOE has selected are structured to complement and to reinforce each other and related efforts. Capitalizing on the links and synergies across the initiatives to meet requirements is a major technical and programmatic challenge.

Transportation Sector. Traditionally, the Department of Transportation (DOT) has conducted the bulk of transportation CIP R&D through the Federal Aviation Administration. This tradition continued with 90 percent of ongoing transportation CIP R&D allocated to aviation security in FY 2002 to date. Other current major transportation CIP R&D efforts include analysis of Global Positioning System (GPS) vulnerabilities; intelligence and security risk assessments, training and awareness, information dissemination; and research on operational methods for improving the performance of transportation systems.

The Interagency Transportation Infrastructure Assurance (TIA) R&D Plan represents a comprehensive approach to assessing threats to the security of the Nation's transportation system and to preparing R&D projects that provide integrated security solutions (e.g., technologies, procedures) tailored to these threats. It addresses the:

- Physical security of transportation modes and intermodal connections (e.g., roads, railroad lines, bridges, tunnels, terminals, locks and dams, piers, etc.);
- Security of vital communications, navigation and information systems and networks (e.g., the Global Positioning System);
- Susceptibility of transportation operators and users to weapons of mass destruction (WMD); and
- Development and dissemination of information about system threats, vulnerabilities, and best practices to transportation system developers, operators, and users.

On February 17, 2002, the Federal Aviation Administration (FAA) was substantially reorganized under Public Law 107–71, the Aviation and Transportation Security Act (ATSA). On that date, the Transportation Security Administration (TSA) assumed all of the FAA's Civil Aviation Security functions, including aviation security research and development. Public Law 107–71, Section 137(b), specifically tasks TSA with issuing aviation security grants. These changes will require new relationships and inter-relationships to be formed.

The DOT mandate for transportation infrastructure assurance focuses on all land, sea and air components, with the added challenge of a diversity of ownership, operators, and governmental responsibilities. The DOT mandate has three main focus areas:

- Assess Vulnerabilities of Interdependent Elements of the Transportation System. This focus area will conduct an overall assessment of transportation supporting infrastructures, their vulnerabilities, and potential impact on transportation in the event of the loss of those supporting infrastructures. This assessment plan will include electric power and telecommunication systems, and it will incorporate related work by the Volpe Center on GPS vulnerabilities and work done in other departments and agencies related to PDD–63, especially the Departments of Energy and Commerce. The report will also include assessments completed by the National Security Telecommunications Advisory Committee.
- Assess Cyber Vulnerabilities of E–Commerce Systems. Shippers, brokers, and customers rely increasingly on accurate and timely information to maximize efficiency in an increasingly global economy. Business-to-business or so-called "B2B" transactions are now the norm. E-commerce and electronic data interchange (EDI) have greatly improved information flow and has become an essential tool for intermodal cargo movements. Yet, by their nature, these information-based systems pose a serious vulnerability for the transportation system. Although progress has been made to identify potential short-term fixes to service and data interruptions, no clear theme or effort has developed within the transportation community to prepare for emerging potentially serious cyber threats. This focus area will assess the emerging vulnerabilities of these systems.
- Evaluate Response Team Requirements. The Department of Transportation is one of several federal agencies with teams that can respond to a terrorist attack. A General Accounting Office (GAO) report in November 2000 ("Federal Response Teams Provide Varied Capabilities") found that "Federal agencies

lack a coherent framework to develop and evaluate budget requirements for their response teams because there is no national strategy with clearly defined outcomes." Under the Federal Response Plan, DOT has responsibilities to coordinate and when necessary provide transportation for all federal resources supporting local response and management of terrorist attacks or natural disasters. During natural disasters, responsibilities of the Research and Special Programs Administration (RSPA) Office of Emergency Transportation (OET) typically include the transportation for shipments of commodities, such as ice, water, generators, and plastic sheeting.

Aviation has a strong history of robust R&D efforts on transportation infrastructure assurance and security, a tradition that will continue. Given surface transportation's importance and vulnerability, as highlighted by several recent studies and high-profile incidents, it is essential to improve surface transportation security, given the emerging 21st Century threats of cyber terrorism, as well as chemical, biological, nuclear, and radiological weapons. The interagency development of the TIA R&D Plan addresses and coordinates these challenging tasks of protecting our nation's transportation infrastructure from terrorist threats. The Plan's next stage will include heightened involvement of private industry in developing and honing transportation infrastructure assurance R&D.

Interdependencies. The economy and national security of the United States are becoming increasingly dependent on a spectrum of U.S. and international infrastructures, which themselves are becoming increasingly interdependent. This trend has accelerated over the last ten years with the adoption of information technology and concomitant infrastructures. And while the U.S. economy has long depended on several critical infrastructures, the coupling among them had historically been rather loose.

In recent years, however, important technological, economic, and regulatory changes have dramatically altered the relationships among infrastructures. At the same time as the information technology revolution led to substantially more interconnected infrastructures, "just-in-time" business practices have reduced margins for error in infrastructure support. Deregulation and growth of competition in key infrastructures has eroded spare infrastructure capacity that served as a useful "shock absorber" in key infrastructures. Furthermore, the growth of mergers among infrastructure providers has led to further pressures to reduce spare infrastructure capacity as management has sought to wring excess costs out of merged companies to realize savings. Any one of these trends would serve as a cause for uneasiness. The collision of all four trends has no precedent in American economic history. While important steps have been taken in individual infrastructures, the issue of interdependent and cascading effects among infrastructures has received almost no attention. Accordingly, a greater understanding of the nature and implications of these infrastructure connections motivates this effort.

Several efforts are underway to try to address issues raised by interdependencies. These efforts include (1) learning about the secure operation of complex interactive networks and systems, and furthering the understanding of the dynamics of complex interactive networks/systems; (2) technology development and vulnerability analysis capability R&D, aimed at analyzing national and defense infrastructures and their critical interdependencies; (3) developing an easy-to-use, deployable state-of-the-art hazard and consequence prediction system.

The National Infrastructure Simulation and Analysis Center (NISAC), a joint Sandia and Los Alamos National Laboratories program under the management of the Defense Threat Reduction Agency (DTRA), has a major effort underway to model, simulate, end analyze interdependent infrastructures and the consequences of these interdependencies.

The major efforts underway, as well as those being investigated for the future, are designed to meet the following research challenges.

- Build a theoretical framework for understanding and predicting the nature of interdependencies and their effects on the country as a whole.
- Develop the capability to model and simulate in real-time the behavior of the Nation's interconnected infrastructures. We can achieve this goal by developing an architecture and related enabling technologies to integrate infrastructure-specific and interdependence databases and analysis tools to study the linkages among the interdependent critical infrastructures, the interdependencies associated with those linkages, their impacts, and their likely causes.
- Develop a set of quantitative metrics for measuring the scale of impacts of interdependency-related disruptions.

- Develop new technologies and techniques to contain, mitigate, and defend against the effects of interdependency-related disruptions, such as escalating, cascading, latent, and cross-infrastructure failures.
- Develop capabilities to adequately and realistically test new methodologies, techniques, and technologies.
- Define a set of tasks for further work on specific national security policy issues that could be analyzed using these tools and methodologies. This work could include, for example, characterizing the potential interdependence implications, from national security and economic perspectives, of current trends within the private sector (e.g., restructuring, deregulation, increased reliance on cyber monitoring and control systems) and their implications for national security; identifying interdependency vulnerabilities in the U.S. economy; and developing metrics for interdependencies.
- Develop the ability to characterize and incorporate new critical infrastructures into the models and methodologies as such infrastructures develop.

Interdependencies among critical infrastructures are what make this set of problems significantly different than those we have faced in the past, and it is what makes them difficult. Government, the national labs, academia, and private industry are doing great work to build an understanding of these issues and tools to solve these problems. Clear challenges lie ahead for government, industry, and academia on which to work together.

Vital Human Services. In early FY 2002, the Environmental Protection Agency (EPA) formed the Water Protection Task Force to manage and coordinate critical water infrastructure protection activities. EPA received supplemental FY 2002 appropriations to support counter terrorism activities in the states and at drinking water and wastewater utilities. Actions underway are:

- to provide direct grant assistance to large, publicly owned drinking water facilities, and to assist large private systems;
- to support development of tools, training, and technical assistance for small and medium drinking water and wastewater utilities; and
- to promote information sharing and research to improve treatment and detection methods.

EPA is awarding direct grants to publicly owned drinking water utilities that regularly serve populations of in excess of 100,000. In addition, EPA is working with the states, tribes, and utility organizations to determine the best ways to meet small and medium system needs through a combination of training, development and distribution of tools, and technical assistance.

Examples of tools under development include: Vulnerability Assessments and Remediation Plan methodology for large drinking water utilities; a Security Vulnerability Assessment Methodology and implementing software for wastewater utilities (VSAT) to be released by the Association of Metropolitan Sewerage Agencies in June 2002; and model Emergency Response Guidelines for both waste and drinking water systems.

The Department of Health and Human Services (HHS) program will focus on the Vital Human Service sector's high priority research and development issues identified by the National Security Council (NSC)-led interagency Critical Infrastructure Coordinating Group. The first R&D issue is the previously mentioned effort to develop a vulnerability assessment methodology for the water supply sector. The second issue is the emergency services infrastructure, which includes studying critical interdependencies between hospital and health care response systems and the communications, essential transportation, public safety, and emergency medical systems. This effort will look at how threats or damage to communications and transportation systems may affect the response capabilities of hospitals and health care communities. A related effort will look at protection of hospital infrastructures, focusing on critical hospital operations in response to a chemical or biological incident including decontamination, preventing cross-contamination, hospital capacity issues, etc.

EPA works with the Centers for Disease Control and Prevention, the Food and Drug Administration, the Federal Bureau of Investigation (FBI) and the Department of Defense to develop information on biological, chemical and radiological contaminants, in particular to respond to their presence in drinking water. One outcome is an assessment of the state of knowledge on technologies to detect contaminants, monitoring protocols and techniques, and treatment effectiveness. The Water Protection Task Force is working with EPA's Office of Research and Development to develop a comprehensive water security research plan.

Outreach. The events of September 11 had a transforming impact on perceptions of the vulnerability of critical infrastructures not only in the U.S. but also abroad. Although the U.S. was the immediate and direct target of international terrorism, many other countries reacted with an understanding that critical infrastructures are globally connected in many ways, which will increase in the future. Interdependence increases the inherent vulnerability of national infrastructures and can make the consequences even more severe. The immediacy of this sense of CI vulnerability has persuaded officials in many nations that they need to take advantage of the best R&D to understand and to solve the problems. They also recognized that no country has a monopoly on the relevant technologies.

After September 11, international cooperation in CIP R&D acquired a new sense of urgency. The U.S. has a compelling interest in making other countries aware of the CIP problems and vulnerabilities and enlisting the best thinking of the international R&D community into the problems. Our partners have an overriding interest in applying best U.S. thinking and practices and establishing a dialogue with U.S. researchers. Over the past year, the U.S. has intensified its existing cooperative CIP R&D activities internationally and has developed new initiatives to take advantage of the emerging consensus.

Finally, the education of the next generation of researchers and professors in information assurance and security technologies is of critical national importance. The Administration has made inroads in this area by introducing scholarship funding into universities across America. The Cybercorps Scholarship for Service program encourages college students to become high tech computer security professionals within the government. Managed by the National Science Foundation and the Office of Personnel Management, this program also helps build academic programs at universities in the area of computer security.

Academia itself has responded to the need for exchange and dialogue among leaders in government, industry, and academia concerning the need for, and utility of, information security and information assurance education through various forums. One example is the Colloquium for Information Systems Security Education (CISSE), a leading proponent for implementing courses of instruction in information security into American higher education. The Colloquium encourages educational institutions to teach appropriate information systems security courses in various curricula to meet the needs of 21st Century consumers and to offer courses to meet the growing demand for information system security professionals.

CONCLUSION

Funding has not always kept pace with requirements for research and development. One example is the Banking and Finance sector in which the task of examining the vulnerabilities and interdependencies of the entire sector requires significant resources beyond initial investment in developing modeling tools.

It is vitally important to recognize that the overall effort to accomplish the federal R&D necessary to address all the identified gaps and shortfalls in critical infrastructure protection R&D is a cooperative effort. Many programs are complementary, and others are joint efforts. Accordingly, funding disapproval for a program in one department ripples across other departments and negatively impacts national goals.

Research and development is a critical component of the Federal Government's efforts to address the critical infrastructure protection challenge. The explosive growth in new technology, particularly in the information infrastructure, requires constant efforts to stay abreast of the new technologies and the new vulnerabilities and threats they bring in their wake.

Mr. Chairman, at this point I would be pleased to answer any questions from the Committee's distinguished Members.

Attachment A

CIP R&D Standing Committee in the S&T Structure of the Executive Branch

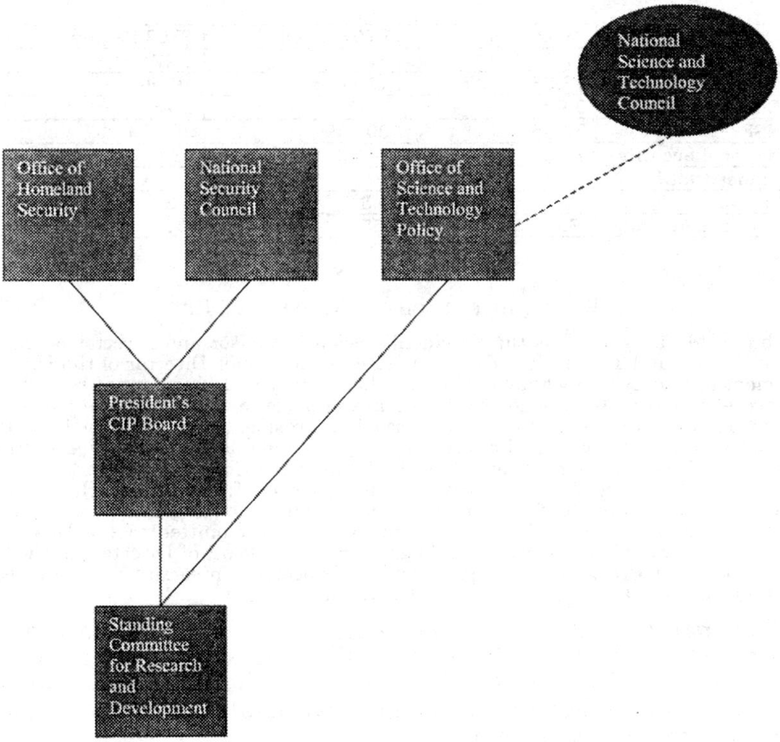

Attachment B.

The budget numbers below reflect funding for CIP R&D programs as reported by OMB.

Dept	FY02 Request	FY02 Enacted	FY03 Request
Agriculture	47.23	47.23	5.47
Commerce	17.55	13.64	16.58
Energy	2.99	2.99	6.75
NSF	52.35	209.69	203.73
National Security	707.5	765.38	633.6
Transportation	8.58	1	1.07
Treasury	13.2	3.3	3.3
Veterans Affairs	.75	.55	.33

BIOGRAPHY FOR JOHN H. MARBURGER, III

John H. Marburger, III is the President's Science Advisor and Director of the Office of Science and Technology. Dr. Marburger is the former Director of the U.S. Department of Energy's Brookhaven National Laboratory and President of Brookhaven Science Associates. He is presently on a leave of absence from the State University of New York at Stony Brook where he served as President and Professor from 1980 to 1994 and as a University Professor of Physics and Electrical Engineering from 1994 to 1997. Dr. Marburger served as the Dean of the College of Letters, Arts and Sciences at the University of Southern California from 1976 to 1980. He has been a member of numerous professional, civic, and philanthropic organizations including the Universities Research Association, the Advisory Committee to the New York State Senate Committee on Higher Education and the Board of Directors of the Museums at Stony Brook. He is a graduate of Princeton University and received a Ph.D. in Applied Physics from Stanford University.

Chairman BOEHLERT. Now we're pleased to have, once again, before the Committee Mr. James K. Kallstrom, special advisor to the Governor, New York State Office of Public Security and a former key official in the Federal Bureau of Investigation and one who has long experience in this field.

Mr. Kallstrom, welcome once again.

STATEMENT OF MR. JAMES K. KALLSTROM, SPECIAL ADVISOR TO THE GOVERNOR, NEW YORK STATE OFFICE OF PUBLIC SECURITY, ALBANY, NEW YORK

Mr. KALLSTROM. Thank you, Mr. Chairman, and thank you Members of the Committee. It's a pleasure to be here. I congratulate you on this hearing. I think it's critically important that the citizens understand some of these issues, the college students understand some of these issues, so that all of us together can find our way through these challenges that we face today and, certainly, will face in the future.

I have some rather lengthy remarks, but I will just abbreviate those, sir, and ask you to include my remarks.

Chairman BOEHLERT. Without objection, so ordered.

Mr. KALLSTROM. According to a joint Computer Security Institute/FBI survey, two-thirds of all security breaches on private networks are still not being reported to relevant authorities. The FBI-authored survey found that although 90 percent of companies admitted that they had identified security breaches in the past 12 months, only 35 percent reported the incidents to law enforcement authorities.

Threats to information networks exist over a range of threat bases scenarios on both the cyber-side, including denial of service and deliberate hacking attacks, and intentional introduction of viruses, such as the I-love-you virus, as well as potential physical attacks on critical cyber infrastructure locations such as transmitting and generating stations.

In general terms, the threats posed to networks and systems in Upstate New York as in the rest of the state have to do with a lack of systems redundancy, a deficiency in the physical security standards of critical cyber infrastructure sites, as well as lack of surplus or custom-made international manufactured components of generators, transformers, and other infrastructure that would result in prolonged system outages and service failure in the event of an attack.

On March 8, 2002, Governor Pataki announced the formation of a cyber security task force, charged with evaluating the state's critical cyber infrastructure, public and private, identifying potential means of cyber attack and devising recommended security practices for private industry, state-operated information systems and the general public.

The diversified skills and knowledge embodied in the cyber terrorism task force, encompass State and Federal Government agencies, the private sector, and academia, and is enabling the state to assess and prioritize the critical cyber infrastructure of greatest concern in terms of interdependencies and vulnerabilities. It is essential that government and academia intersect with the private sector to avoid duplication of efforts in terms of Federal grants and development projects, as well as to productively utilize the trillions of dollars annually invested in research and development to better secure business processes, protection of intellectual and physical property as well as employees' safety.

Both the Governor and the Office of Public Security support the Cyber Security Research and Development Act introduced by your committee and yourself, Mr. Chairman, to establish new programs and increase funding levels for computer and network security research and development, build cyber security research centers that draw together academia and industry, as well as to report to Congress on critical infrastructure weaknesses.

The current mission of the Office of Public Security is closely utilizing NYSTAR, which is a New York State private sector technology initiative, as a source of new technology developed by homegrown New York companies that enhances the security of our citizens as well as contributes jobs and revenues to the state. Through NYSTAR's involvement with the New York Office of Public Security, a New York based company has installed biometric fingerprint scanners—and I might say with the new technology of ultrasound that looks below the skin to the actual dermis where the fingerprints are actually produced. It's quite interesting technology.

And we've introduced those to select airports here in the state, Kennedy in particular, as part of Governor Pataki's announcement of heightened aviation security measures that he introduced in April. Should the technology continue to prove effective, there is a strong possibility of further deployment at the other New York airports and perhaps nationwide.

A major area of concern that is currently hindering homeland security efforts in our state and in our country is the existence of outdated public disclosure laws both at the state and Federal level. This directly contributes to an unwillingness by public and private sector infrastructure operators to share key critical and vulnerability related information with the government due to the fear of public exposure under Federal FOIA and New York's FOIL law.

It is hoped that the passage of the President's recently submitted Homeland Security Legislation—containing provisions that would exempt from disclosure information provided voluntarily by non-federal agencies or individuals—that relates to infrastructure vulnerabilities or other vulnerabilities to terrorism will protect against disclosure that places our citizens at risk.

Critical infrastructure protection and the gathering and dissemination of useful, actionable counterterrorism intelligence are totally linked as concepts. To this end, it is vital that middleware be developed and implemented that successfully integrates the state's 29 agency databases offering single query and response capabilities.

So that our first line of defense in this state, our state and local law enforcement, can make a query late at night some night on the Taconic Parkway or any other road or any other place in the state and actually find out the significance of the query they are making, past the normal MCIC checks into the databases that hold so much information of relevance to counter-terrorism. And, of course, the need to integrate Federal databases has been well documented both in Congressional proceedings and in the media and certainly is fully endorsed by the state and the Office of Public Security.

Mr. Chairman, I will be happy to take questions. I have many, many more details of the summary I just gave in my prepared remarks. Again, I want to thank you for holding this hearing. I think it's timely, it's relevant, and it produces information here in sort of the heart of New York State that the public needs to know.

Chairman BOEHLERT. Thank you very much, Mr. Kallstrom, and your entire statement will be in the record. And please convey to the Governor my personal appreciation and appreciation of the Committee for his strong support for our Cyber Security Research and Development Act. We're moving in the right direction on that.

Mr. KALLSTROM. Yes, sir, without question.

Chairman BOEHLERT. Thank you for your expert testimony.

[The prepared statement of Mr. Kallstrom follows:]

PREPARED STATEMENT OF JAMES K. KALLSTROM

Good Morning Chairman Boehlert and distinguished Members of this Committee. On behalf of Governor George E. Pataki, I want to thank the Members of this Committee and in particular you, Mr. Chairman, for your strong leadership in this area of global significance. Your efforts to ensure that New York State is well armed to battle the cyber war will not only benefit the citizens of this great State, but also will be a beacon for the rest of the Nation to follow. I appreciate the opportunity to share with you the position of New York State in the discussion "Homeland Security: The Federal and New York Response."

The tragic events of September 11, 2001 have forever changed the things that we understood to be absolute truths on September 10ih. There will be—and must be—much change as we move into this new, uncharted world.

Never before has the ability to communicate, gather intelligence, and protect public safety been as heightened as it is now and technology will be the focus of many of these efforts. Technology played an important role in responding to the terrorist attack of September 11th. While technology was a tremendous asset in responding, the use of technology may also be one of the threats in any future event. The use of technology as a weapon of mass destruction is almost a certainty.

New York State has learned from the tragic events of September 11th. We have critically examined our emergency response capabilities, reviewed the policies, procedures, and priorities that currently exist within our information technology infrastructure and assessed where we need to go from here. By learning the lessons from the past, as well as working and training together for future responses, we can better prepare to meet the challenges that will face us all in this new era. Our efforts are focused on four phases: Prevention, Detection, Response and Recovery.

I'd like to take this opportunity to discuss some of the efforts that are underway in New York State, which have been reinforced by some of our lessons learned.

Are we prepared?

The people of New York State have responded heroically to the terrorist events of September 11, 2001. As we respond to the physical nature of terrorism, we cannot lose sight of the realities and threats posed by acts of cyber terrorism.

New York State, along with the rest of the world, has become a 24/7 operation, by means of the communications evolution brought about chiefly by the Internet. This evolution enhances availability of essential services, economic opportunity and accessibility of private citizens, businesses, and government, *anywhere and at any time*. But this constant, "online" way of life also increases our vulnerability to cyber threats.

During our preparation for the Year 2000 date change, New York State was acutely aware that cyber terrorism could be used as a weapon of mass destruction. As technology continues to evolve, a greater percentage of the primary operations of sensitive utility, communications and banking infrastructure will continue to shift from manual to online controls. Accordingly, the threat posed by a determined terrorist with technological and computing skills will grow, in terms of capability to disrupt critical information flows in communications, capital movement and allocation, as well as the operation of critical utilities that affect the lives of millions of New Yorkers and the economy of the Region, Country and World.

However, a federal statutory definition of what constitutes a Weapon of Mass Destruction (WMD) is too traditional and narrow. Title 50 U.S.C. Section 2032(1), in part defines a WMD as *"any weapon or device that is intended, or has the capability, to cause death or serious bodily injury to a significant number of people through the release, dissemination, or impact of toxic or poisonous chemicals or their precursors; a disease organism; or radiation or radioactivity."*

The use of technology to inflict damage to our critical infrastructures must be officially recognized as a potential WMD. Areas of potential impact on the State include: catastrophic loss of life, disruption of essential services, and incapacitation/destruction of critical infrastructure. To be successful in this war on terrorism, we must not allow our thinking to be constrained by the traditional definitions of inflicting destruction.

Technology can be used to cause a similar level of physical destruction as traditional methods of WMD. At a Critical Infrastructure conference two years ago, Richard Clarke, now the President's Special Advisor for Cyber Security, predicted the occurrence of a major cyber attack directed at the United States.

What makes technology as a weapon of mass destruction so fearful is the fact that: (1) Cyber attacks can originate from anywhere; (2) There is a lack of qualified and trained personnel to detect and respond immediately to these attacks; and (3) There are no formal means of signaling an alert to the rest of the country.

We don't have to look at the international scene to discover potential sources of cyber attacks; the potential is right here at home. A single individual, operating out of a private residence and using commercially available hardware and software, is capable of perpetrating acts which could bring about the economic and social chaos described above.

One of New York State's newest and biggest challenges will be responding to attacks on public and private sector computer networks and information systems. Those at greatest risk are the networks and systems linked to state and national critical infrastructures, including utilities, communications, banking, energy, and transportation.

In this global e-transaction climate, our society must be ever vigilant in preparing to defend itself against the myriad of threats posed by cyber terrorism to human safety, as well as economic prosperity. We must strive to make improvements in both the physical and cyber components of our infrastructure.

In general terms, the threats posed to networks and systems in upstate New York are the same as those faced by the rest of the Nation; cyber terrorism knows no geographic boundaries.

New York State is developing a plan to identify the vulnerabilities of, and potential threats to, our critical infrastructures and assets from the use of technology as a WMD.

The State's critical infrastructure and assets, public and private, are as vast and diverse as the State's topography. Some of the more prominent sectors include:

1. **Telecommunications**;
2. **Utilities:** electric, gas, water, waste, steam, nuclear;
3. **Government:** towns, villages, cities, counties, school districts, State, and Federal;
4. **Public Safety/Emergency Preparedness:** 911, police, fire, emergency managers;
5. **Health:** hospitals, nursing homes, pharmacies, health clinics, home care providers;
6. **Financial/Economic:** stock exchange, banks, investment firms;
7. **Transportation:** signal/guidance systems of rail, airline, bus, trucking, shipping/handling companies;
8. **Education:** University labs and research facilities;
9. **Food:** agriculture and dairy processing industry; and
10. **Technology.**

However, input is required from the private as well as the public sectors to identify all of the critical infrastructures, assets, and interdependencies that the State needs to protect.

Will the State be prepared if the following threat basis scenarios are realized?

1. Air traffic control equipment malfunctions;
2. Heating, ventilation, and air conditioning systems are modified to circulate harmful gases with in a large office complex, containing a population equivalent to a small city;
3. 911 telephone communications are interrupted;
4. Electrical blackouts occur;
5. Power dam water flow is modified to allow downstream flooding incomparable to any previous natural disaster;
6. Financial markets are disrupted.

What if these attacks were programmed to occur at the same time?

Fighting cyber terrorism requires a coordinated approach, uniting local resources with those at the State and national level. Additionally, New York State must fit into a coordinated national plan, which ensures that staffing, equipment, and training resources are maximized, and provides a mechanism to share vital information in real-time. The magnitude of the impact of potential cyber attacks is impossible to predict. Because of this uncertainty, the State must have plans in place that anticipate likely scenarios and address them in a way that reduces the capabilities of terrorists to endanger the health, welfare and security of our State.

Recognizing these vulnerabilities, on March 8, 2002, Governor Pataki announced the formation of a Cyber Security Task Force, charged with evaluating the State's critical cyber infrastructure identifying potential means of cyber attack, and devising recommended security practices for private industry, State-operated information systems and the general public.

The diversified skills and knowledge embodied in the Cyber Security Task Force, encompassing State and Federal Government agencies, the private sector and academia, is enabling the State to assess and prioritize the critical cyber infrastructure of greatest concern.

Government laboratories, centers of higher learning and private sector entities are all working to advance the current state of technology in data-mining, encryption, search and query capability, natural language analysis and other capabilities that enable information gathering and interoperability between databases and operating systems. It is equally essential that government and academia work closely with the private sector to ensure we maximize efforts in terms of development of projects and competing for Federal, State and private resources to protect our information systems.

The aim of the Governor and the Office of Public Security in creating this Task Force is quite simple. We seek to prevent harm to life, destruction of critical infrastructure and denial of essential services, all of which could result from a cyber attack. Accomplishing this mission will be fundamentally more challenging. The anonymity that characterizes cyberspace, coupled with the abundance of technologically skilled individuals who wish to do our country harm, represent the darker aspects of an invention that has enhanced education, commerce and communications to unprecedented degrees.

In answering this challenge, we have assembled a diverse, thoroughly qualified group that encompasses the White House Office of Cyber Security, select government agencies of New York State, corporate representatives of the New York City Partnership, and New York University's centers of high-technology learning and research, as well as the State University of New York. We are confident that this Task Force is fully capable of presenting a broad, informed perspective on identifying and prioritizing the industry sectors of greatest concern, discerning potential mechanisms of cyber attack, and devising appropriate detection, response and recovery protocols.

As part of the Task Force's efforts to strengthen the relationship between the public and private sectors, a subgroup within the Task Force is working to establish a comprehensive database of technology vendors who could be called upon during a time of emergency to lend critical resources and assets to the State as needed.

The Task Force is also identifying principle points of contact in all sectors to conduct inventories and risk assessments and identify best practices and standards for measuring preparedness against cyber terrorism threats.

Security Has Been a Number One Priority of Governor Pataki Prior to the Date Change (Y2K)

Governor Pataki has long been active in ensuring that appropriate response mechanisms are in place in the event of a disaster—whether it be natural or otherwise. He made information security a priority during Y2K. In this regard, Governor Pataki placed a priority on the activities of the State Disaster Preparedness Commission and most recently established the Office of Public Security.

The Office of Public Security was created to ensure central coordination of all State activities related to public security and close coordination with the Homeland Office of Governor Ridge in Washington. These activities have proven critical in our ability to respond to September 11, and for any future event that may occur.

In the areas of physical security, we have established a statewide critical infrastructure workgroup that has gathered detailed information about the State's critical infrastructure, and is developing strategies for protecting it, including scenario simulation exercises.

In the area of information security, we are addressing this on a number of fronts. In early 2000, the Governor established the State's first statewide Information Security Office to provide a coordinated, comprehensive approach to developing policies and procedures to protect the State's critical technology infrastructures, such as networks and data centers. The policy required every agency to have an information security officer.

In addition, the Information Security Office is enhancing the State's intrusion detection and vulnerability scanning abilities. The Office is establishing cooperative Security partnerships within State agencies, and other entities. Currently, we are sharing information security data with 60 State agencies and a number of other states.

A major concern that severely hinders our efforts is outdated public disclosure laws, both at the Federal and State levels. Critical public and private sector entities will not share sensitive information with the government out of well-founded fears that it will later have to be publicly disclosed under either the federal Freedom of Information Act (FOIA), or the New York State Freedom of Information Law (FOIL). Utilities, telecommunications, transportation and computer-based organizations view these laws as weak and reliance on them, at best, uncertain in this context. The President's recently submitted draft legislation, which would create the Department of Homeland Security, contains provisions that would exempt from required disclosure by the new Department, "information provided voluntarily by non-Federal agencies or individuals that relates to infrastructure vulnerabilities or other vulnerabilities to terrorism" (Section 204). Although this proposal is certainly a step in the right direction, more must be done to provide adequate assurances that sensitive information about potential threats to the Nation's critical infrastructure, both cyber and physical, will not fall into the wrong hands just to be turned around and used to attack our citizens. Indeed it is for this reason that Governor Pataki recently submitted legislation to amend our State's FOIL law to exempt sensitive information from disclosure that is "obtained or complied in monitoring, investigating or preparing for terrorist activity." This bill passed our State Senate last week and is currently pending in the Assembly in Albany.

In an age where detailed maps and drawings of sensitive infrastructure locations are turning up in the caves of Afghanistan, in al Qaeda training camps, it is unacceptable to the exercise of responsible government to release information relating to structural design, performance specifications or physical/cyber vulnerability of key public infrastructure to persons or entities without a legitimate need to know.

We are now living in the world of wireless communications. Our first responders, however, use incompatible and often obsolete radio equipment-complicating their ability to communicate with each other. In fact, runners are often still used for communication by first responders in emergencies.

New York State is currently requesting proposals for a Statewide Wireless Network. Using state-of-the-art technology, this new radio system will provide both voice and data communication capability. In crisis situations, where seconds count, all responders, police officers, fire personnel, EMS and EMTs, should be able to instantly communicate with each other. We are also ensuring redundancy and backup capabilities through our statewide communications initiative.

Under the new system, New York State will provide the necessary backbone infrastructure for a statewide emergency communications system which localities may join at their option, based on each individual locality's needs. The Statewide Wireless Network is committed to pursing partnership arrangements with government organizations to ensure maximum interoperability, reduce overall costs of the system, and reduce the time necessary for implementation.

But it is crucial to look beyond New York State's jurisdictions and boundaries, to assure that interoperable communications with the first-responders of neighboring states are enabled. In an age where wireless communications, including for emergency response, are increasingly becoming the common form of communication, the Federal Government must be cognizant of issues regarding interoperability between our borders as well as frequency allocations.

As Mr. Joe Allbaugh, Director of FEMA, testified on October 16, 2001 to the United States Senate, "if there is a single item that we could do, (it) is to make sure that police, fire, emergency responders can communicate with one another. Oftentimes, I go into a community and there are all types of bands and frequencies used and folks, literally, who are responding to an incident can't talk to one another."

The bravery and courage of our firefighters, police and other emergency responders to the horrific events of September 11th has given special meaning to the word "heroes." If we are to protect their lives and safeguard the public we serve, we must provide these and other heroes across the State with the ability to communicate effectively and quickly with each other.

Governor Pataki's number one priority directive to the Office of Public Security is to detect and prevent any future terrorist attacks against our State or country. One of the keys to prevention is to better inform and educate State and local police—70,000 strong in New York State alone and more than 650,000 nationwide. New York is addressing the issue of information sharing with law enforcement with the implementation of New York State's Counter-Terrorism Network (CTN)—the first of its kind in the Nation—to provide critical intelligence in the war on terrorism to local law enforcement personnel statewide. This network, announced by Governor Pataki in January 2002, allows critical counter-terrorism information culled from various government sources to be shared instantaneously with local law enforcement via a secure computer network.

Governor Pataki's philosophy with regard to technology has always been one of collaboration and mutual coordination—developing strong public and private partnerships.

"We can't do it alone; our successes are collective efforts."

Any such coordinated effort must bear in mind the first responders are at the local level. Federal and State government need to be in a position to assist and support, not impede these efforts.

We need to build on the foundation that has already been established—and works well—from the local emergency offices, to the state emergency operations center, to the federal emergency office. We must not add more layers that make effective response more difficult.

By working collaboratively across all levels of government, we can achieve success and provide an even-more significant response.

Thank you for the opportunity to be here this morning.

BIOGRAPHY FOR JAMES K. KALLSTROM

Senior Policy Advisor to the Governor for Counter-Terrorism

Mr. Kallstrom was born May 5, 1943, in Worcester, Massachusetts, and completed his early education in Massachusetts. He graduated from the University of Massachusetts at Amherst in 1966, and subsequently served in the United States Marine Corps, during the Vietnam War, attaining the rank of Captain.

Mr. Kallstrom entered on duty with the FBI as a Special Agent in February 1970 and following a period of training, was assigned to the Baltimore, Maryland FBI Office. In 1971, he was transferred to the FBI's New York Office.

In July 1976, Mr. Kallstrom assumed supervisory duties in the New York Division. In May 1981, Mr. Kallstrom was appointed as the Chief of the Special Operations Branch; a position he held until December 1990.

In December 1990, Mr. Kallstrom was promoted to Section Chief of the Engineering Section, Technical Services Division, FBI Headquarters, the position he held until September 1993, when he was promoted to Special Agent in Charge of the Special Operations Division, New York Division. The Special Operations Division is responsible for all technical and surveillance operations in support of all FBI investigative programs.

In February 1995, Mr. Kallstrom was designated the Assistant Director in Charge, New York Division, a position he held until his retirement on December 31, 1997.

Mr. Kallstrom is currently a Senior Executive Vice President and Management Committee Member with MBNA America located in Wilmington, Delaware.

On October 10, 2001, Mr. Kallstrom took a leave of absence from MBNA America and was appointed Director of the newly created New York State Office Of Public Security by Governor George E. Pataki. In May 2002, Mr. Kallstrom was appointed Senior Advisor to the Governor for Counter-Terrorism. As Senior Advisor, Mr. Kallstrom is responsible for coordinating and bolstering anti-terrorist efforts throughout the State of New York. He reports directly to the Governor and serves as a member of the Governor's senior staff.

Mr. Kallstrom is married to the former Susan Aver of Riviera Beach, Maryland and they have two daughters, Erika age 22 and Kristel age 17.

Chairman BOEHLERT. Next is Mr. John Tritak, Director of White House Critical Infrastructure Assurance Office.

Mr. Tritak, welcome.

STATEMENT OF MR. JOHN S. TRITAK, DIRECTOR, WHITE HOUSE CRITICAL INFRASTRUCTURE ASSURANCE OFFICE (CIAO), WASHINGTON, D.C.

Mr. TRITAK. That's why we call it CIAO.

Chairman BOEHLERT. CIAO. Explain that, so Critical Infrastructure.

Mr. TRITAK. Critical Infrastructure Assurance Office, which was a creation of the foundation's committee report.

Chairman BOEHLERT. Now for the word CIAO, Mr. Tritak.

Mr. TRITAK. I also am a New Yorker from Rochester, so I think we're ganging up on Mr. Engle here. I don't know if he's a New Yorker or not.

It's a pleasure to be here. I would like to have my written remarks entered into the record so I can focus on some of the key themes that I'm picking up on and build on the point that you were making earlier, Mr. Chairman, about why this matters to all of us, not just the experts in Washington or in Albany.

When I got into graduate school in 1985, national security was something the Federal Government did more or less by itself. It was a top down concept. The role of private industry was to either build the tools for defense or to provide a tax base.

Same thing goes for the average citizen. Indeed, national economic security used to refer largely to free trade, access to markets overseas and raw materials. In fact, if you look at the national organization, there is a National Economic Council and a National Security Council, and there was some overlap but not a lot.

Now we're seeing something changed; 9/11 brought that home. We're seeing a convergence between national and economic security into now homeland security.

And why is that the case? Because the economy itself is under attack. Our way of life is under attack. Osama Bin Laden made it very clear. He called upon his supporters to use all means necessary to attack the pillars of the American economy. Why? Because what they are essentially driving us to do is to withdraw from our role and responsibilities overseas and to change the very nature of our culture and our society. They are going to fail, but that doesn't mean they are not going to try again.

Also the homeland security proposition presents a new form of problem. For the first time in our history, it's a problem the Federal Government can't solve alone. All the planning we're doing, all the resources we're putting into this, the creation of a whole new Homeland Security Department as a vital important step toward safeguarding our homeland isn't going to be enough by itself, and that is because, of course, our economy and our infrastructure are largely privately owned and operated.

So we're seeing a paradigmatic shift, really, from a top down to a combination of top down, bottom up. What that means, essentially, is that we need to redefine and clarify the respective role and responsibility of government and industry and the public in securing our homeland.

And as I indicated, the Administration is taking a very important step in creating this new department. There is a balancing act that needs to always to be struck between coordination on the one hand and consolidation on the other. I think the balance that's being struck now is exactly right. In fact, my office will be part of that new department when it is created, hopefully within this year.

But as much as we talk about the role of the Federal Government, I think 9/11 demonstrated very clearly as Governor Ridge said recently, "Homeland security—if you want to secure the homeland, secure the hometown."

In the final analysis, national homeland security is a state and local and community based effort. The fact that we survived this horrible catastrophe was because of the brilliant leadership that was exercised at the State level—Governor Pataki, Mayor Giuliani, the first responders, the Secret Service and the private sector that did an enormous amount of contingency planning prior to that event. And had they not done so, you couldn't have stood on Wall Street on the Monday after the Tuesday bombing. It was an example, a case study, in exactly what critical infrastructure assurance is all about. And I applaud the efforts of New York and the leadership that has been demonstrated by Governor Pataki and the City of New York.

Let me go back to a point I made just a few moments ago, which is, "Use all means necessary." Well, that translates to mean exploit vulnerabilities wherever you can find them. On 9/11, they exploited the vulnerabilities of our commercial air system and converted commercial airliners into cruise missiles. But they are not going to limit themselves to the physical world. They are going to exploit vulnerabilities where they can find them and cyberspace is clearly an area that they are going to exploit. We know. We have found information about Al Qaeda which suggests that they were going to try to disrupt the function of the digital control systems to affect water supply.

You know, most people think about cyberspace and they almost think it's something that is removed from them, quite literally. It's something that resides and takes place in the ethersphere. It doesn't reach out and touch us, but we're not really talking about digital hygiene here. What we are talking about is something that very much and increasingly will touch our lives in a very physical and demonstrable way.

What if, God forbid, we had another attack and what if, in combination with a terrible bomb, we also had our 911 emergency services communications disrupted? You can just imagine—I have talked to Mr. Kallstrom and others who provided emergency services in their former lives—that it would be a mess and a lot more people would die. So cyberspace can reach out and touch us.

It's also a vulnerability we can't get away from. It's a function of being connected, interdependent and relying on the Internet. The exploitation is not just in technology. It's not just about software. It's the combination of technology meshed into business processes and run by human beings, and vulnerabilities can be found in any of those places, which is why this is essentially a business risk management problem.

To make it a little more complicated, the tools of mass destruction that cyber capabilities can provide are not the monopoly of nation states or even terrorist groups. They are widely distributed throughout the world, and there are very, very talented people out there who can do enormous harm from their home under certain circumstances, which is why it is so difficult to talk about threats.

In many cases we have to start with vulnerabilities, vulnerabilities that could disrupt critical services, and for us to determine to what extent those critical services rely on information systems and networks and what are the consequences of those vulnerabilities being exploited. It's a very different way of thinking about it. In the old days, we used to measure threats by looking at it through spy glasses or counting tanks or whatever.

Here, we have to look at capabilities and potential vulnerabilities. This is why it's a CEO problem not a CIO problem. This is about how people run their businesses and the extent to which they are relying on the ever-extending digital nervous system to provide these critical services.

And that is why we need to develop the base of our capabilities to rectify the imbalance that gives the attacker the advantage over the defender. That's why we need to improve our information sharing both within the private sector and between the government and private sector, which is why we need to increase the number of skilled IT security professionals and improve opportunities for undergraduates.

There are 23 centers of excellence in IT security. Let us say four of those institutions are here in New York: Syracuse, Polytechnic University, SUNY–Buffalo and SUNY–Stony Brook. We need more advanced degrees in academic tracks so that we can cultivate the underlying information infrastructure, if you like, that builds these capabilities, incorporates them into our business schools and our legal (inaudible).

Last year, there were only eight people awarded Ph.D.s in information security. And that is why, also—and to echo the words of Dr. Marburger, why we need to move forward in R&D. First, because we want to think about the next information super highway or digital nervous system, designing a way that actually incorporates into the basic design secure communications.

It is also important to develop model simulation capabilities so we can figure out how disruptions in one area can manifest themselves as disruptions in other areas. We're never going to get this through actuarial data. We hope we never get to that point. We need to understand where those disruptions lie and manage the risks associated with them.

Obviously, I've thought a lot about this subject, and I know I've also run out of time so I will stop there, except to say it's a pleasure to be here and welcome the opportunity to be here today as well as answer any questions you may have later.

Chairman BOEHLERT. Thank you very much for that excellent testimony.

[The prepared statement of Mr. Tritak follows:]

PREPARED STATEMENT OF JOHN S. TRITAK

Mr. Chairman, Members of the Committee, I am honored to appear before you today to discuss cyber terrorism and information assurance. It is very clear in this current environment that the country needs a single, unified homeland security structure that will improve protection against today's threats and be flexible enough to help meet the unknown threats of the future.

In his address to the Nation on June 6th, President Bush stated that he intended to create a Department of Homeland Security to ensure that he continues to carry out his most important responsibility as President of the United States—that of protecting and defending the American people. His decision to take this monumental step—the most sweeping reorganization of our national security establishment in over 50 years—was made on the basis of careful study and experience gained since September 11. The Administration considered a number of organizational approaches for the new department proposed by various commissions, think tanks, and Members of Congress.

The new Department of Homeland Security would be organized into four divisions: Border and Transportation Security; Emergency Preparedness and Response; Chemical, Biological, Radiological and Nuclear Countermeasures; and Information Analysis and Infrastructure Protection. The new department will be comprised mainly of existing organizational elements located in other Federal departments and agencies. For example, my office, the Critical Infrastructure Assurance Office (CIAO), now located in the Department of Commerce's Bureau of Industry and Security, will become part of the new Information Analysis and Infrastructure Protection division.

I would like to take the opportunity now to provide some background on the CIAO and to discuss briefly some of the specific activities and initiatives we are currently undertaking on behalf of cyberspace security and homeland security.

What are the Components of the Nation's Critical Infrastructure?

The United States has long depended on a complex of systems critical infrastructures to assure the delivery of vital services. Critical infrastructures comprise those industries, institutions, and distribution networks and systems that provide a continual flow of the goods and services essential to the Nation's defense and economic security and to the health, welfare, and safety of its citizens.

These infrastructures are deemed "critical" because their incapacity or destruction could have a debilitating regional or national impact. These infrastructures relate to:

- Information and communications
- Electric power generation, transmission, and distribution
- Oil and gas production and distribution
- Banking and finance
- Transportation
- Water supply
- Health and Human Services
- Emergency government services

Critical infrastructure assurance is concerned with the readiness, reliability, and continuity of infrastructure services (which rely on physical and cyber-based assets) so that they are less vulnerable to disruptions, so that any impairment is of short duration and limited in scale, and that services are readily restored when disruptions occur.

To complicate matters further, each of the critical infrastructure sectors is becoming increasingly interdependent and interconnected. Disruptions in one sector are increasingly likely to affect adversely the operations of others. We are witnesses to that phenomenon now. The cascading fallout from the tragic events of September 11th graphically makes the business case for critical infrastructure protection. That the loss of telecommunications services can impede financial service transactions and delivery of electric power is no longer an exercise scenario. There can be no e-commerce without "e" electricity. There can be no e-commerce without e-communications.

Our society, economy, and government are increasingly linked together into an ever-expanding national digital nervous system. Disruptions to that system, however and wherever they arise, can cascade well beyond the vicinity of the initial occurrence and can cause regional and, potentially, national disturbances.

Primary Threats to Critical Infrastructure Components

Threats to critical infrastructure fall into two overlapping categories:

- Physical attacks against the "real property" components of the infrastructures; and
- Cyber attacks against the information or communications components that control these infrastructures.

Assuring delivery of critical infrastructure services is not a new requirement. Indeed, the need for owners and operators to manage the risks arising from service disruptions has existed for as long as there have been critical infrastructures.

What is new are the operational challenges to assured service delivery arising from an increased dependence on information systems and networks to operate critical infrastructures. This dependence exposes the infrastructures to new vulnerabilities.

The cyber tools needed to cause significant disruption to infrastructure operations are readily available. Within the last three years alone there has been a dramatic expansion of accessibility to the tools and techniques that can cause harm to critical infrastructures by electronic means.

One does not have to be a "cyber terrorist" or an "information warrior" to obtain and use these new weapons of mass disruption. Those who can use these tools and techniques range from the recreational hacker to the terrorist to the Nation state intent on obtaining strategic advantage.

From the perspective of individual enterprises, the consequences of an attack can be the same, regardless of who the attacker is. Disruptions to the delivery of vital services resulting from attacks on critical infrastructures thus pose an unprecedented risk to national and economic security. What if the recent computer viruses Code Red and Nimda had hostile payloads in them and did more than just threaten the stability, reliability and dependability of the Internet?

Securing the Nation's critical infrastructures against cyber attacks presents yet another difficult problem. The Federal Government cannot post soldiers or police officers at the perimeters of telecommunications facilities or electric power plants to keep out digital attackers. There are no boundaries or borders in cyberspace.

Background on the Critical Infrastructure Assurance Office

The CIAO is not a recent arrival to the homeland security effort: we have been diligently working to realize the objective of critical infrastructure assurance for four years. Specifically, the CIAO was created in May 1998 by Presidential Decision Directive 63 (PDD–63) to serve as an interagency office located at the Department of Commerce to coordinate the Federal Government's initiatives on critical infrastructure assurance.

On October 18, 2001, Executive Order 13231 (the Order), was issued and entitled "Critical Infrastructure Protection in the Information Age," the CIAO began serving as a member of and an advisor to the newly created President's Critical Infrastructure Protection Board (the Board). The Board was created to coordinate Federal efforts and programs relating to the protection of information systems and networks essential to the operation of the Nation's critical infrastructures. In carrying out its responsibilities, the Board fully coordinates its efforts and programs with the Assistant to the President for Homeland Security.

Major Activities and Initiatives

CIAO's responsibilities for developing and coordinating national critical infrastructure policy focus on three key areas: (A) promoting national outreach and awareness campaigns both in the private sector and at the State and local government level; (B) assisting Federal agencies to analyze their own risk exposure and critical infrastructure dependencies; and (C) coordinating the preparation of an integrated national strategy for critical infrastructure assurance.

A. Outreach and Awareness

The Federal Government acting alone cannot hope to secure our nation's critical infrastructures. The national policy of infrastructure assurance can only be achieved by a voluntary public-private partnership of unprecedented scope involving business and government at the Federal, State, and local levels. Forging a broad based partnership between industry and government lies at the heart of the CIAO's mission.

1. Private Sector Partnerships

CIAO has developed and implemented a nationwide industry outreach program targeting senior corporate leadership responsible for setting company policy and allocating company resources. The challenge of such an effort is to present a compelling business case for corporate action. The primary focus of the CIAO's efforts continues to be on the critical infrastructure industries (i.e., information and communications, banking and finance, transportation, energy, and water supply). The basic thrust of these efforts is to communicate the message that critical infrastructure assurance is a matter of corporate governance and risk management. Senior management is responsible for securing corporate assets—including information and information systems. Corporate boards are accountable, as part of their fiduciary duty, to provide effective oversight of the development and implementation of appropriate infrastructure security policies and best practices.

In addition to infrastructure owners and operators, the CIAO's awareness and outreach efforts also target other influential stakeholders in the economy. The risk management community including the audit and insurance professions—is particularly effective in raising matters of corporate governance and accountability with boards and senior management. In addition, the investment community is increasingly interested in how information security practices affect shareholder value—a concern of vital interest to corporate boards and management.

In partnership with these communities, the CIAO has worked to translate potential threats to critical infrastructure into business case models that corporate boards and senior management can understand. Corporate leaders are beginning to understand that tools capable of disrupting their operations are readily available not merely to terrorists and hostile nation states but to a wide range of potential "bad actors." As a consequence, they are beginning to grasp that the risks to their companies can and will affect operational survivability, shareholder value, customer relations, and public confidence.

The CIAO has also worked actively to facilitate greater communication among the private infrastructure sectors themselves. As individual Federal lead agencies under PDD–63 formed partnerships with their respective critical infrastructure sectors, private industry representatives quickly identified a need for cross-industry dialogue and sharing of experience to improve the effectiveness and efficiency of individual sector assurance efforts. In response to that expressed need, the CIAO assisted its private sector partners in establishing the Partnership for Critical Infrastructure Security (PCIS). The PCIS provides a unique forum for government and private sector owners and operators of critical infrastructures to address issues of mutual interest and concern. It builds upon, without duplicating, the public-private efforts already being undertaken by the Federal Lead Agencies.

2. State and Local Government Partnerships

The CIAO has developed an outreach and awareness program for State and local governments to complement and support its outreach program to industry. State and local governments provide critical services that make them a critical infrastructure in themselves. They also play an important role as catalyst for public-private partnerships at the community level, particularly for emergency response planning and crisis management. The issue of securing the underlying information networks that support their critical services was a relatively new issue before September 11. State and local governments tend to be well organized as a sector, with multiple common interest groups.

Similar to its program for industry, the CIAO has laid out a plan to implement outreach partnerships with respected and credible channels within State and local government. CIAO has also met with the National Governors Association and the National Association of State Chief Information Officers to encourage input into the National Strategy for Cyberspace Security.

The front lines for the new types of threats facing our country, both physical and cyber, clearly are in our communities and in our individual institutions. Smaller communities and stakeholders have far fewer resources to collect information and analyze appropriate actions to take. Consequently, in February of this year, the CIAO began a series of four state conferences on Critical Infrastructures: Working Together in a New World, designed to collect lessons learned and applied from the events of September 11 from New York, Arlington, and communities across the United States. The intent of this conference series is to deliver a compendium of community best practices at the end of the first quarter of 2003. The first conference was held in Texas and the second in New Jersey. The last two will be held in the latter part of 2002 and the first quarter of 2003.

3. Education

The CIAO has worked with The National Education and Training Program (E&T) for Infrastructure and Information Assurance (IIA) to strengthen the cadre of Information Technology professionals who protect our computer networks, cyber infrastructures, management information systems, and the information stored in them. It also provides additional areas of knowledge through education, training and awareness initiatives to all constituency areas or groups that are relevant to infrastructure and information assurance education and training.

The E&T program encompasses three initiatives:

- Increasing the capacity of our nation's colleges and universities to educate students in information assurance;
- Training current Federal information technology practitioners in IIA recommended practices; and,
- Increasing the awareness of IIA responsibilities in our schools and communities.

Central to the first initiative is the "Cybercorps: Scholarship for Service" (SFS) program. SFS provides grants to selected 4-year colleges and universities to develop or improve their capacity to train information assurance professionals. It also provides selected 4-year colleges and universities scholarship grants to attract students to the information assurance and computer security fields.

B. Support for Federal Government Infrastructure Activities

1. Homeland Security Information Integration Program

The Administration is proposing in the President's Fiscal Year 2003 budget request to establish an Information Integration Program Office (IIPO) within the CIAO to improve the coordination of information sharing essential to combating terrorism nationwide. The most important function of this office will be to design and help implement an interagency information architecture that will support efforts to find, track, and respond to terrorist threats within the United States and around the world, in a way that improves both the time of response and the quality of decisions. Together with the lead federal agencies, and guided strategically by the Office of Homeland Security, the IIPO will: (a) create an essential information inventory; (b) determine horizontal and vertical sharing requirements; (c) define a target architecture for information sharing; and (d) determine the personnel, software, hardware, and technical resources needed to implement the architecture. The foundation projects will produce roadmaps (migration strategies) that will be used by the agencies to move to the desired state.

2. Federal Asset Dependency Analysis—Project Matrix

The CIAO also is responsible for assisting civilian Federal departments and agencies in analyzing their dependencies on critical infrastructures to assure that the Federal Government continues to be able to deliver services essential to the Nation's security, economy, or the health and safety of its citizens, notwithstanding deliberate attempts by a variety of threats to disrupt such services through cyber or physical attacks.

To carry out this mission, the CIAO developed "Project Matrix," a program designed to identify and characterize accurately the assets and associated infrastructure dependencies and interdependencies that the U.S. Government requires to fulfill its most critical responsibilities to the Nation. These are deemed "critical" because their incapacitation could jeopardize the Nation's security, seriously disrupt the functioning of the national economy, or adversely affect the health or safety of large segments of the American public. Project Matrix involves a three-step process in which each civilian Federal department and agency identifies (i) its critical assets; (ii) other Federal Government assets, systems, and networks on which those critical assets depend to operate; and (iii) all associated dependencies on privately owned and operated critical infrastructures.

Early experience with the CIAO's Project Matrix process has demonstrated such significant utility that the Office of Management and Budget has recently issued a directive requiring all Federal civilian agencies under its authority to fund and perform the analysis.

C. Integrated National Strategy for Critical Infrastructure Assurance

Threats to critical infrastructure fall into two overlapping categories: (1) physical attacks against the "real property" components of the infrastructures; and (2) cyber attacks against the information or communications components that control these infrastructures. PDD–63 charged the CIAO, as secretariat for the National Coordinator, to integrate infrastructure assurance plans developed by each of the individual infrastructure sectors into a comprehensive "National Infrastructure Assurance Plan." In January 2000, the CIAO coordinated the release of the *National Plan for Information Systems Protection, Version 1.0* which articulated a complex interagency process for approaching critical infrastructure and cyber-related issues in the Federal Government. As a consequence of the events of September 11, however, the President restructured the responsibilities for developing strategies to respond to these two categories of threats.

The attacks on the World Trade Center and the Pentagon underscored the need to devote greater attention to securing and defending against the threat of physical attack upon our nation's homeland. To address this need, the President, on October 8, 2001, established the Office of Homeland Security and charged it "to develop and coordinate the implementation of a comprehensive national strategy to secure the United States from terrorist threats or attacks." In view of the scope of the mission assigned to the Office of Homeland Security, the President separately created the President's Critical Infrastructure Protection Board and gave it responsibility for "ensur[ing] protection of information systems for critical infrastructure, including emergency preparedness communications, and the physical assets that support such systems." In keeping with this mission, the Board is developing a national strategy for cyberspace security.

In the post-September 11 environment, the CIAO continues to play its role to coordinate and facilitate input from private industry—and now, State and local government—to the national strategies on critical infrastructure protection. The Office of Homeland Security has enlisted the CIAO to provide coordination and support for its efforts to compile information and private sector input to its strategy to protect the physical facilities of critical infrastructure systems. Our office, working with the Lead Agencies and our private sector partners including PCIS, has been instrumental in coordinating input from the private sector to the cyberspace security strategy.

Information Sharing

Encouraging the appropriate exchange of information within and among the infrastructure sectors and between the sectors and government provides infrastructure operators with a more accurate and complete picture of their operational risks, as well as the techniques and tools for managing those risks. It is also an invaluable tool to enable the government to direct resources to assist the private sector and to undertake appropriate law enforcement and other activities against wrongdoers.

Our security as a nation depends on our collective ability to understand vulnerabilities, detect incidents, prevent attacks, protect essential infrastructures, and, as necessary, rapidly respond and reconstitute systems. Moreover, the amount of information collected by industry and government agencies is potentially overwhelming. Millions of probes are launched everyday on our nation's networks. Some of these represent actual attempts at intrusion.

The government can help by being more specific about the characteristics of information it finds most useful to reduce the burden of information sharing on private businesses and help them to manage it. A recent initiative by *CXO Media,* in partnership with the NIPC and the U.S. Secret Service, to streamline reporting forms for voluntary sharing of data by industry reflects the type of private-public partnership that is possible. Unfortunately, even with that result, the same concerns that are the subject of this hearing surfaced in public comment when the product was rolled-out.

We have seen progress, however. Industry sees Information Sharing and Analysis Centers (ISACs) as providing a benefit. Five of the eight critical infrastructure sectors identified in PDD–63 have created ISACs to identify threats and vulnerabilities within their industries and prevent them from escalating and disrupting business operations. Moreover, through the Partnership for Critical Infrastructure Security (PCIS) various industries have engaged in cross-sector dialogues to examine interdependencies, multi-sector information sharing, legislative and public policy issues, research and workforce development, and industry participation in the preparation of the national strategies for homeland and cyberspace security. Collectively, these activities improve the overall effectiveness of sector assurance efforts.

Conclusion

The American economy is the most successful in the world. However, the same technological capabilities that have enabled us to succeed can now also be turned against us in the information age. Corporate assets and infrastructures can be exploited and turned against the American people, as we witnessed in the events of September 11th. Powerful computing systems can be hijacked and employed to launch attacks that can disrupt operations of critical services that support public safety and daily economic processes. In such an environment, sharing information is essential to both government and industry to make better-informed decisions and to take more timely and effective action.

In the post-September 11 environment, the CIAO continues to play its role to coordinate and facilitate input from private industry—and now, State and local government—to the national strategies on critical infrastructure protection. The Office of Homeland Security has enlisted the CIAO to provide coordination and support for its efforts to compile information and private sector input to its strategy to protect the physical facilities of critical infrastructure systems.

Thank you for the opportunity to appear before you today. At this time I welcome any questions that you may have.

BIOGRAPHY FOR JOHN S. TRITAK

John S. Tritak is Director of the Critical Infrastructure Assurance Office (CIAO). Mr. Tritak is a member of the President's Critical Infrastructure Protection Board and is responsible for coordinating the development of the Administration's National Strategy for Critical Infrastructure Protection to address threats to the Nation's communications and electronic systems, transportation, energy, banking and finance, health and medical services, water supply, and key government services. He is also responsible for assisting Federal departments and agencies in identifying their dependencies on critical infrastructure under the Project Matrix program, and coordinating national awareness and outreach efforts to private industry and State and local governments.

Before joining the CIAO, Mr. Tritak was an attorney with the law firm of Verner, Liipfert, Bernhard, McPherson and Hand, Chartered. As a member of the firm's federal practice group, Mr. Tritak provided advice and counsel on wide range of legal, legislative and policy matters, including critical infrastructure protection, to domestic and international clients in the defense, telecommunications, and transportation industries.

Mr. Tritak served as Deputy Director for Defense Relations and Security Assistance in the State Department's Bureau of Politico-Military Affairs, where he was responsible for coordinating U.S. efforts in security assistance and defense trade in

Europe, Africa, and the Middle East. As Deputy Director of the Bureau's Office of Policy Analysis, he advised on matters relating to postwar Persian Gulf security.

He also served as a State Department adviser to the U.S. delegation negotiating the Strategic Arms Reduction Treaty in Geneva, Switzerland, and was a deputy political adviser to U.S. Central Command in Riyadh, Saudi Arabia, during Operation Desert Shield. Mr. Tritak previously served as a consultant on national security and military matters at Pacific Sierra Research.

Mr. Tritak received a B.S. in political science from the State University of New York at Brockport, an M.A. in War Studies from the University of London, Kings College, and earned his J.D. from the Georgetown University Law Center.

Chairman BOEHLERT. And, finally, the fourth member of the panel, Dr. James Engle, Deputy Undersecretary for Science and Technology, United States Air Force.

Dr. Engle.

STATEMENT OF DR. JAMES B. ENGLE, DEPUTY UNDERSECRETARY FOR SCIENCE AND TECHNOLOGY, UNITED STATES AIR FORCE, ARLINGTON, VIRGINIA

Dr. ENGLE. Thank you very much, Mr. Chairman, Members of the Committee and staff. I really appreciate being here today particularly because this is my first opportunity to testify before your committee, and I'm pleased that you chose this setting to do it in, close to what I would consider a world class institution that's doing this kind of research as we speak; and I would say leading not only our nation, but our world in the types of work that we need to do to answer some of the serious questions that your committee poses.

The Rome Lab up the street here has world class people, world class facilities and, I think, our science is some of the best that you can find anywhere on Earth. So I am particularly pleased to be here today to participate in this hearing and answer any questions you have.

The Air Force is fortunate in many regards because we have a very focused enterprise in which we bring to bear our science and technology. And it's important that you understand the difference between the focus of our technology and what the needs of the Nation are at this particular time, because, as was pointed out by earlier comments from our panel, those particular arrangements between the institutions and our government are changing, and that will no doubt involve the United States Air Force, as well.

But because we are at a focused kind of enterprise, we tend to bring our vision about our technology there on the capabilities of what the war fighter needs and, in our case, that vision has to do with integrated air and space capability for rapid and decisive global engagement. To do that, of course, we need secure and assured information to do our work effort at all times.

As a matter of introduction, although most of our work is focused in this direction—and I'll tell you briefly about some of that—most of that technology is easily translatable and transferable to a broader sector of our government as well as to our academic and investor partners across the United States, and we are aggressively pursuing those kinds of activities to make sure that the knowledge that we gain here at Rome is available to a broader audience.

The Air Force must be prepared to counter a worldwide availability of advance weapons, regional instabilities, global terrorism, as we talked about, and other emerging and less predictable asymmetrical threats. An awful lot of our work focuses on that kind of activity.

As you know, we recently completed a complete review of our science and technology program and we established six long-term challenges that focus that research, and, they include finding and tracking, command and control, controlled effects, what we call sanctuary, rapid aerospace response, and effective aerospace persistence.

Embedded in every one of those capabilities is a requirement for, again, assured and dependable information to our war fighter. That underpins why we have such a strong and robust investment in this particular area, and let me just talk briefly about that.

As we speak, remarks on the Hill are very promising for this particular area as there is great enthusiasm from Congress to increase our funding levels in this area. But even before that, in the President's budget that was sent across for '03, we are up about 15 percent in our investment in this particular area. That equates to roughly an investment almost to a third of what was mentioned earlier. We are investing about $240 million a year in this area if you consider the totality of what we consider information, which includes our command and control assets, as well. So it's not just strictly in the security part of this or in the information assurance part but across the whole information domain that we place emphasis on in the Air Force. We are approximating about a quarter of a billion dollars of investment.

We are very selective about our investment in that we try to focus it on the highest priorities that we need at the particular time. In some cases, in particular in the area of command and control, it's kind of an emergency because of our efforts in Afghanistan right now and we have done some remarkable work post 9/11 to get there.

We are also closely working and are the executive agent for a number of DARPA, the Defense Advanced Research Projects Agency, activities and intelligence community in a number of leading edge activities that will bring, I think, substantial improvements to our ability to secure our networks.

We also do a considerable amount of outreach to universities and industry, and we also have a partnership for research excellence in transition with SUNY Buffalo, Carnegie Mellon, Boston University and other universities.

In addition, we really applaud your work with 3394. I think that that will significantly help fill in the gaps in our computer security technology research and information assurance work force development, something that we are desperately in need of, as well.

In the specific areas of information assurance and cyber security, the Air Force system requires the following capabilities, and we focus on research in these areas: first, the ability to transfer information across heterogenous or coalition networks; our ability to test and exercise information operation of personnel, equipment, tactics and doctrine in a realistic setting; the ability to assess the risk of information systems; and, finally, the automatic ability to globally correlate and fuse attack information.

As you can tell from those, we are aggressively pursuing some technologies that will assist us in all of those areas, and I think that that will be translatable also to a broader audience.

There are many more things I can tell you about the specifics of what we're going to do, but typically protecting our enterprise requires capability to assure defense against a wide variety of attacks and threats. Detecting attacks requires early warning. We will work on that. Assessing attacks requires the capability to identify the adversary, and, again, a lot of work in that area and responding to attacks. I don't have time to cover these in detail and the specific activities that we have underway, but they are covered in my testimony for your review, and I will make them available to you, as well as, I believe, that you will have a chance to see some of these firsthand this afternoon.

In combating terrorism, in the post-9/11 attack, of course, most of our focus was drawn to our activities in Afghanistan where we are aggressively committing a lot of our work, although I want to point out that a lot of our science and technology was really addressing this kind of threat even before 9/11; and although our priorities are changing as a result of that incident, I think that you will find that the Air Force overall has a very robust set of investments in helping protect the Nation in this kind of threat.

And I would conclude, since I am out of time already, that the Air Force is very aggressive in this area, as you know. Our people are first rate. We do share the concern that your committee has with the production and the stability of our work force, the production of talented people in our country that we can use for our research and development. We have a number of aggressive programs underway to recruit and to encourage our young people to seek degrees in information assurance and information activities in our universities.

We are actively recruiting in that way and provide sponsorship for scholarships, and I believe that those will help not only the United States Air Force but our nation in the long-term.

However, our institution by itself is probably not sufficient to ensure the level of participation in this industry that we need, and any help that your committee can give us will be much appreciated, particularly the bill that you have just gotten through the Congress.

So I conclude with that, and I am very pleased to be here and would be more than happy to answer yours and the Committee's questions.

[The prepared statement of Dr. Engle follows:]

PREPARED STATEMENT OF JAMES B. ENGLE

Mr. Chairman, Members of the Committee, and Staff, I very much appreciate the opportunity to provide testimony on the Fiscal Year 2003 Air Force Science and Technology (S&T) Program and, in particular, our focus on information technologies including information assurance and cyber security. The United States Air Force is committed to a robust S&T Program that enables us to achieve our vision of an integrated air and space force capable of rapid and decisive global engagement. Our goal is to retain our dominance of air and space in future conflicts against both traditional and asymmetrical threats, including the protection of Air Force information assets from terrorist activities.

Innovation is a vital part of our heritage and is key to ensuring the Air Force will meet the challenges of tomorrow. Focusing our warfighting capabilities towards this end will involve continued innovations in how we think about employing our forces to defend our nation. A robust S&T Program is the foundation of this vision. The Air Force must be prepared to counter the worldwide availability of advanced weapons, regional instabilities, global terrorism, and other emerging and less predictable asymmetrical threats. We focus our technologies on those critical enduring capabilities that will ensure we will always be ready for an uncertain future. These are our Long-Term S&T Challenges and they include: Finding and Tracking; Command and Control; Controlled Effects; Sanctuary; Rapid Aerospace Response; and Effective Aerospace Persistence.

S&T BUDGET

Recognizing that S&T is a key contributor to transformation, the Air Force is working hard to increase S&T funding, while maintaining a balanced S&T portfolio. The Air Force Fiscal Year 2003 President's Budget (PB) request was $1,659 million, an increase of approximately $280 million over the Fiscal Year 2002 PB. Of this amount, the information technology investment (including information assurance and cyber security) increased approximately 15 percent over the information technology baseline program.

In conjunction with the PB increase, there has been a significant increase in the involvement of the warfighting commands and senior Air Force leadership in S&T planning, programming, and budgeting. For example, we have established periodic S&T Summits where the Secretary of the Air Force, the Air Force Chief of Staff, and the Air Force four-stars and other senior leaders review the S&T portfolio. The latest S&T Summit focused on transformational technologies that can be developed to assist in combating terrorism and homeland defense.

S&T PLANNING PROCESS

I am pleased to report that the S&T Planning Review we undertook and completed in response to Section 252 of the National Defense Authorization Act for Fiscal Year 2001, Public Law 106–398, was an overwhelming success. We approached this review enthusiastically and received the wholehearted support and participation of not only the Air Force S&T community, but also the requirements, planning, logistics, and user communities. The need for increased investment in information technology, to include information assurance and cyber security, was highlighted in both the short-term objectives and long-term challenges that were identified as part of this comprehensive review. We have already defined technology development roadmaps for each of these objectives and challenges, and are continuing to address them in our S&T Program. In fact, the results of this S&T Planning Review are now providing both a short-term and long-term focus to the S&T Program, and are being incorporated into the Air Force S&T Plan, the Air Force Strategic Plan, and are laying the foundation for future Air Force S&T budget planning.

MAXIMIZING OUR S&T DOLLARS

The Air Force continues to leverage technology to increase combat effectiveness. Our strategy is to pursue integrated technology solutions that support our warfighter's highest priority capability needs. We also pursue fundamental enabling technologies that support tomorrow's Air Force systems, including both information assurance and cyber security. We have sponsored a number of information assurance and cyber security workshops. These workshops have participants from academia, other government agencies, and industry and have shaped our information assurance and cyber security research program.

We are very selective about investing in the highest priority information assurance and cyber security technological opportunities. We constantly seek opportunities to integrate Air Force planning and leverage our S&T funds by cooperating with other Services, Agencies, the private sector, and international partners. The Air Force also has strong interagency efforts in information assurance and cyber security technology developments. We work closely with and are the executing agent for a number of the Defense Advanced Research Projects Agency (DARPA) and intelligence community information technology programs. For example, we are the technical agent for DARPA's Fault Tolerant Networks program. This program is developing technologies that provide continuous correct network operations even through cyber attack. Additionally, the Air Force has established strategic alliances with universities and industry to further leverage and coordinate S&T investments in information technologies. For example, in the area of information fusion, we have established three Partnerships for Research Excellence and Transition (PRETs) efforts with SUNY Buffalo, Carnegie Mellon, and Boston University. The PRETs are collaborative research efforts between our laboratory, the university and an industry partner with the goal to perform and transition research in higher-level information fusion.

A venue that could help the Air Force fill in the gaps in computer security technology research and information assurance workforce development is the "Cyber Security Research and Development Act" (H.R. 3394; S. 2182). This proposed legislation could fund multidisciplinary research; foster increased collaboration among government, academia and industry; and support the development of information assurance professionals from technicians to researchers. As the Nation increases emphasis on computer security technology, the Air Force will be able to leverage both the larger pool of information assurance professionals and the university researchers working on information assurance and cyber security technology needs.

Another venue that could facilitate transition of maturing information assurance and cyber security technologies is the Congressionally-directed Challenge Program. This program as described in Section 244, "Program to Accelerate the Introduction of Innovative Technology in Defense Acquisition Programs," of H.R. 2586, directs the Office of the Secretary of Defense to increase the introduction of innovative and cost-saving technology in acquisition programs.

As technological superiority is a perishable commodity, we work hard to maximize the payoff of our S&T funding. We do this by not only developing transformational technologies, but also by speeding the introduction of these new technologies into new capabilities for our warfighters using spiral development and reduced acquisition cycle times.

INFORMATION ASSURANCE AND CYBER SECURITY

The Air Force's information infrastructure must be highly automated, adaptive, and resilient to attacks of all types. Based on emerging operational concepts, Air Force systems require the following capabilities: ability to transfer information across heterogeneous and coalition networks at varying security classification and compartment levels in a secure and reliable manner; ability to perform operations, such as assessing and maintaining the confidentiality, integrity, and timeliness of information systems; ability to test and exercise information operations personnel, equipment, tactics, and doctrine in a realistic operational environment to include red teaming; ability to assess the risk to information systems and determine courses of action; and the automatic ability to globally correlate and fuse attack information from multiple sensors to determine the origin, nature, and scope of an information warfare attack. These needs stress every aspect of information assurance and cyber security technology and systems concepts currently being researched and developed by the Air Force.

The Air Force operates globally, thus our global information enterprise consists of data, information, and networks made up of commercially available communications augmented by military communication systems when required. Our information assurance program vision is to protect the Air Force information enterprise with a high degree of confidence, detect information attacks, assess information attacks, and respond to a successful information warfare attack on our information assets. Protecting this enterprise requires the capability to assure defense against a wide variety of threats and the ability to manage risks. Detecting attacks requires early warnings using cooperating sensors, and efficient, accurate data reduction, fusion, and correlation techniques. Assessing attacks requires the capability to identify the adversary, determine mission impacts, and develop courses of action. Finally, responding to an attack requires the capability to gracefully degrade, recover, and reconstitute our information systems, while providing feedback to improve our protection and detection processes. Our technical approach, full spectrum information technology program, is to balance our investment across all four areas.

In order to achieve full spectrum information assurance and cyber security, we collaborate with other researchers and our Air Force operational community. Examples of our operational partnerships include Air Combat Command, Air Intelligence Agency, National Imagery Mapping Agency, and the Intelligence Community. Our research partnerships include DARPA, the Army Research Laboratory, and the Naval Research Laboratory. Additionally, the Air Force has recently established the Information Assurance Institute with Cornell University. This collaborative research institute provides university researchers access to our information assurance technology needs and facilities and our scientists and engineers access to Cornell's technical experts. Further, the Air Force supports the establishment of "The National Center of Excellence for Information and Infrastructure Assurance" in the Rome, New York, area. The Center will be a partnership between government, academia, and industry, with the focus on multidisciplinary research to enhance, protect, and defend information systems.

Threats to our information systems are increasing. Our adversaries are getting more sophisticated and have access to the same commercially available hardware and software as we do. For example, there are many software tools available on the

Internet to "hack" into systems. Our biggest challenges include better detection techniques, intrusion tolerance, and forensic response.

The Air Force needs to be able to detect cyber attacks, such as hidden information, distributed attacks over time and machines, and insider attacks. In the area of intrusion tolerance, we need to be able to continue to operate our global information enterprise while under attack. This requires that our warfighters have the capability to accurately identify cyber attacks. Forensic response requires the capability to collect evidence before, during, and after the attack. The Air Force S&T community, especially our Information Directorate here in Rome, New York, is leading the way in several areas of this research. I would like to describe just a few.

Steganography, derived from the Greek word meaning "covered writing," is a military communication tactic used since ancient times. The objectives of steganography are to develop the means to hide information from an adversary, while denying him this same capability. The Air Force S&T Program has efforts in both areas—detecting hidden information and hiding undetectable information. Our scientists and engineers, working in collaboration with academia and industry, have developed and demonstrated techniques to detect and hide information in a number of digital imagery formats. We are actively working on extending these techniques to other multimedia formats.

As Air Force systems start to deploy wireless information technology, it is also important for us to understand the potential new information system threats. Under the President's Critical Infrastructure Protection initiative, we were able to extend our information technology program to wireless technology. Based on some results of experiments on wireless Local Area Networks (LANs), the Department of Defense changed implementation policy for LANs and formed a wireless working group, with active Air Force participation.

A recent S&T information technology accomplishment was the demonstration of the Automated Intrusion Detection Environment Advanced Concept Technology Demonstration (ACTD). As the technology lead, the Air Force demonstrated the ability to integrate and correlate sensor data and provide automated warnings to the established incident response reporting structure. It has recently been demonstrated at multiple Department of Defense sites.

A recent information technology transition was the Imagery Support Server Environment (ISSE) Guard program, which provides multi-level security by connecting networks and system of different security classification levels. The ISSE Guard program provides secure, bi-directional transfer of information between these two systems. It is currently being used in our Air Operations Center allowing information transfer between coalition partners.

COMBATING TERRORISM

Since the September 11th attack on the United States, the Air Force has responded to civil and military requests for assistance providing information technologies. For example, an information technology that has been deployed to support Operation Enduring Freedom is the Interactive Data Wall. Think of it as a very large computer screen. The data wall starts at waist level, goes up three feet, and is twelve feet wide. It has very high resolution, with over four million pixels in the display, and can overlay multiple sets of information and show several different displays simultaneously. Anything that can be displayed on a computer or television can be displayed on the data wall. You control the displays through voice recognition software and laser pens. The Air Force has been experimenting with data walls in joint exercises over the past two years and has met with much success in learning how best to use them. In December, the Commander of the Army 10th Mountain Division requested a data wall for immediate deployment in support of Operation Enduring Freedom with a second data wall to follow 90 days later. We delivered the first data wall the next day and the second one in less than 90 days.

WORKFORCE

The Air Force civilian and military S&T workforce is highly motivated and productive. The Air Force is unique in that 20 percent of its laboratory scientist and engineer (S&E) government workforce is active duty military. This gives us a direct link to the warfighter. Some of these military S&Es come directly from operational commands, while others will serve in operational commands later in their careers.

The Air Force is committed to shaping its S&E workforce with the vision to enhance excellence and relevance of S&T into the 21st Century and appreciates the support Congress has provided. Recruiting and retaining information experts is a significant challenge for the Air Force. The number of experts completing college is rather small and the demand for their expertise is high. This challenge requires the Air Force to maintain a dominant edge in technology and also requires us to provide clear direction and growth for our S&E workforce. However, we as do others, find it is difficult to recruit and retain S&Es. The Air Force has several initiatives that address recruitment and retention issues.

The Air Force published a "Concept of Operations for Scientists and Engineers in the United States Air Force" and baselined the requirement for the Air Force S&E workforce. Upon analyzing the baseline requirement, we found our military and civilian authorizations to be about right, but our actual demographics are seriously short in some key areas. We are, therefore, shifting our focus to retaining the workforce we have and infusing it with the vitality of new S&Es to meet tomorrow's need. During the next seven years, we are investing nearly a third of a billion dollars to support the containment and growth of our technological workforce. We are encouraging this growth through critical skills accession bonuses, critical skills retention bonuses, recruiting, and re-recruiting efforts. As we grow our S&E workforce, we are providing career guidance and mentoring that will enable us to meet our 21st Century challenge. Initiatives, such as the special hiring legislation authorized by Congress, which provides "DARPA-like" hiring authority to the military departments, should also provide positive results in shaping our S&E workforce. This authority has only recently been delegated to the Air Force, but we are very optimistic about its potential.

The Air Force strongly supports legislation submitted by the Administration to provide alternative personnel system authority for the Department of Defense. This authority is essential if the Department is to expand and extend the flexibilities now afforded by some in the defense laboratory community under various personnel demonstration projects. Uncertainty in the national security environment requires appropriate flexibility in human resources management.

CONCLUSION

The Air Force is in the midst of a technological and organizational change that is radically altering air and space contributions to the nature of war. We are making important strides in information technologies, including command and control, information assurance, and cyber security in support of an integrated Expeditionary Air and Space Force.

In conclusion, the Air Force is fully committed to providing this nation with the advanced air and space information technologies required to meet America's national security interests around the world and to ensure we remain on the cutting edge of system performance, flexibility, and affordability. The technological advantage we enjoy today is a legacy of decades of investment in S&T. Likewise, our future warfighting capabilities will be substantially determined by today's investment in S&T. As we face the new Millennium, our challenge is to advance secure and responsive information technologies for an Expeditionary Air and Space Force. The Air Force is confident that we can lead the discovery, development, and timely transition of affordable, information technologies that keep our Air Force the best in the world. As an integral part of the Department of Defense's S&T team, we look forward to working with Congress to ensure a strong Air Force S&T Program tailored to achieve our vision of an integrated air and space force.

Mr. Chairman, thank you again, for the opportunity to provide testimony on this very important issue, and thank you for your continuing support of the Air Force S&T Program.

BIOGRAPHY FOR JAMES B. ENGLE

James B. Engle, a member of the Senior Executive Service, is Deputy Assistant Secretary of the Air Force for Science, Technology and Engineering, Washington, D.C. In this position, he is the senior Air Force official responsible for preparing policy and guidance for science and technology; select research, development, and test and evaluation programs; systems engineering; weapons systems pollution prevention; and industrial practices. Mr. Engle develops and directs the managing of programs for research, development, test and evaluation activities, and industrial preparedness and standardization. In addition, he directs Air Force-owned industrial facilities. He also serves as chairman of the Air Force Scientist and Engineer Career Program Policy Council.

Mr. Engle graduated from the University of Arizona in 1970. Two years later, he received a Master's degree in genetics. Mr. Engle retired from the Air Force in the rank of colonel in May 2000, and entered the Senior Executive Service the same month.

EDUCATION:

1970—Bachelor's degree in biology, University of Arizona
1972—Master's degree in genetics, University of Arizona

1975—Squadron Officer School, Maxwell Air Force Base, Ala.
1982—Air Command and Staff College, Maxwell Air Force Base, Ala.
1984—Armed Forces Staff College, Norfolk, Va.
1993—Air War College, Maxwell Air Force Base, Ala.
2000—Program for Senior Executives in National and International Security, Harvard University, Cambridge, Mass.

CAREER CHRONOLOGY:

1. 1973–1974, student, undergraduate pilot training
2. December 1975–October 1977, C–130E/H pilot, 774th Tactical Airlift Squadron, Dyess Air Force Base, Texas
3. November 1977–May 1981, C–130E instructor pilot; standardization and evaluation pilot; and chief of wing tactics, 37th Tactical Airlift Squadron, Rhein-Main Air Base, West Germany
4. June 1981–July 1983, biology instructor and course director, U.S. Air Force Academy, Colorado Springs, Colo.
5. August 1983–December 1984, student, Armed Forces Staff College, Norfolk, Va.
6. January 1985–May 1987, planning and programming officer and Executive Officer to the Air Force Inspector General, Headquarters U.S. Air Force, Washington, D.C.
7. June 1987–December 1989, operations officer and Commander, 1402nd Military Airlift Squadron, Andrews Air Force Base, Md.
8. January 1990–July 1992, section coordinator, Force Programs Section, and Military Assistant to the Supreme Allied Commander Europe, Supreme Headquarters Allied Powers Europe, Mons, Belgium
9. August 1992–June 1993, student, Air War College, Maxwell Air Force Base, Ala.
10. July 1993–May 1995, Commander, 374th Tactical Airlift Operations Group, Yokota Air Base, Japan
11. June 1995–May 1996, Deputy Director of Modeling, Simulation and Analysis, Deputy Chief of Staff for Plans and Programs, and Executive Officer to the Air Force Chief of Staff, Headquarters U.S. Air Force, Washington, D.C.
12. June 1996–April 2000, Chief, Future Concepts Development Division, Directorate of Strategic Planning, Deputy Chief of Staff for Plans and Programs, Headquarters U.S. Air Force, Washington, D.C.
13. May 2000–March 2002, Deputy Director of Strategic Planning, Deputy Chief of Staff for Plans and Programs, Headquarters U.S. Air Force, Washington, D.C.
14. April 2002–present, Deputy Assistant Secretary of the Air Force for Science, Technology and Engineering, Washington, D.C

AWARDS AND HONORS:

Defense Meritorious Service Medal
Legion of Merit with oak leaf cluster
Meritorious Service Medal with oak leaf cluster
Air Force Commendation Medal

PANEL I: DISCUSSION

Chairman BOEHLERT. Thank you very much, Dr. Engle.

I will start off the questioning and I'll adhere to the five-minute rule and then we'll have subsequent rounds if they appear necessary.

And my remarks, understandably, will have a more New York focus, which is one of the reasons why we are all gathered here. I want to pay particular attention to our opportunities that we have right here.

CURRENT AND FUTURE ROLES OF DOD LABORATORIES

Which leads me to ask of you, Dr. Marburger, you know the DOD plays a critical role in protecting infrastructure and in infrastructure R&D. Do you think DOD laboratories, such as the one you've just heard so eloquently talked about by Dr. Engle at Rome—

should they have a greater role to play? Would you envision a greater role in the future, and would that be your recommendation?

Dr. MARBURGER. DOD laboratories have enormous capabilities. And laboratories like AFRL have reoriented themselves in tune with modern needs, needs of modern military and, indeed, needs of the Nation.

I'm very impressed with what's happened with AFRL. I think the program clearly has national significance, not just for the state, and could be the center of the development of cyber security at the economy here in New York.

I do think it's important for DOD to continue to invest in these vital technologies and in the training and recruitment of professionals in them, and my office would encourage continued development of these capabilities.

COLLABORATION BETWEEN CIVILIAN AGENCIES AND THE MILITARY

Chairman BOEHLERT. I have a specific instance in my mind where you can help. Recently, I brought Jane Garvey, the Administrator of the FAA, up to Rome to meet with the people there at the research laboratory, and she was bedazzled, really impressed with what she saw, and they established a good relationship.

But then there's the commingling of funds and the need to get more money for this type of activity to pursue mutual R&D interest, so I think there are important FAA needs in cyber security, but budgets for cross agency collaborations are somewhat constrained, so I think we've got to think out of the box in the future.

Should the Administration consider a dual use R&D initiative to foster such collaboration between civilian agencies and the military to fight cyber terrorism?

Dr. MARBURGER. Well, in the first instance, I believe the creation of the Department of Homeland Security will be an immense step forward in the coordination of some of these activities.

In the cyber area, I think about a half dozen different small organizations will be brought together under the Department of Homeland Security to address this coordination problem. Joint research programs already exist, and one of the functions of this complicated committee structure that I have described in my testimony was to make sure that the different agencies perform complementary parts of this.

But I agree with you, Mr. Chairman, that coordination is a problem, and nothing short of the kind of dramatic consolidation that the Department of Homeland Security represents can address it.

Chairman BOEHLERT. Yes, that's why the President's initiative is being so warmly received in terms of the creation of this new department.

The old way of doing things was for civilian agencies to be over here doing their thing and the military agencies being over in DOD doing their thing and never talking to each other. That's got to change. So as we go through the new budget cycle, Dr. Marburger, I can assure you that the Committee will be very interested in working with you, talking about collaborative activities.

Which brings me to thank Dr. Engle very much. I know this isn't your first visit nor would I expect it will be your last visit up here.

But each time you come up to visit the Rome research site, you tell me how impressed you are with what you see there and I applaud that and I want to keep impressing you and to the tune of encouraging your extra effort as we get more resources for Rome lab to continue the important work that it is doing.

Let me ask Mr. Kallstrom, if I may. You mention the cyber security task force created by Governor Pataki. You talked with us on the Committee before about that. Can you tell us if you have established any sort of relationship with the Air Force Research Laboratory at Rome and taken advantage of what we have there?

Mr. KALLSTROM. We actually haven't done that yet, but it's in our plan. Actually, it's phase two. We're going to bring in a lot more additional technology groups and academic groups.

Chairman BOEHLERT. You will be on the tour with us today.

Mr. KALLSTROM. Yes, sir, that's right.

Chairman BOEHLERT. That's one of the reasons. I mean, there's a hidden agenda here. We don't always have the agenda as published.

Mr. KALLSTROM. We have more of a basis—you know, first level, second level basis to actually acquire the information industry by industry, site by site first, and then maybe phase two will be to apply some—once we have our best practices to then bring in the scientific community.

Chairman BOEHLERT. I think you will be very favorably impressed, Mr. Kallstrom. We talked about this before.

Mr. KALLSTROM. Absolutely.

Chairman BOEHLERT. Part of the hidden agenda is to get you here physically.

Mr. KALLSTROM. Right.

Chairman BOEHLERT. And we're going to get up there together and look at that outstanding facility and get more familiar with some of the people there because it's going to open up whole new vistas for you.

Mr. KALLSTROM. As you probably know—and I don't mean to belabor this—but I think John made the point. A good portion of our critical infrastructure today, for communications, for the power grid, is privately owned and privately managed. And to me, there is no bigger national security asset than the power grid of the United States and the communications grid, if you think about the downside of losing that in any particular community or any particular state.

So we're wrestling with the notion of actually having the operators of those facilities have a discussion with us and others in the government as to what the vulnerabilities of those sites are, both from a cyber standpoint and from a physical standpoint.

THE FREEDOM OF INFORMATION ACT (FOIA): AN IMPEDIMENT TO COLLABORATION?

As I pointed out, they are very reluctant to do that because of the freedom of information laws which are a great law for another purpose. But for the purpose of making public critical information regarding the critical infrastructure, the lawyers in those companies are of the opinion that that information might not survive those laws.

So we're having a very difficult time in actually coming to the table and actually having the type of discussions that we actually need. So we're encouraging—we've spoken to everybody we can in Washington about this issue. It's not just a state issue. It's a Federal issue, also. So that we can—in this new environment, you know, private companies and private citizens and the government are all having to work together. This is a classic case of where a law that was created for great reasons, you know, doesn't quite fit. You know, we need a little bit of a carve out so that we can come together and better protect the infrastructure.

Mr. TRITAK. I would like to comment on that.

Chairman BOEHLERT. Mr. Tritak.

Mr. TRITAK. The point that Mr. Kallstrom made is very important. Companies and the government actually disagree over whether or not the existing FOIA actually protects that information or not. I think it's really the wrong question.

Basically, what we're hearing from companies is that you are asking us to do this because you say it is in the public interest. If it's in the public interest, why aren't you creating a statutory environment that actually promotes and advances voluntary activity of the kind that actually serves the public good? Not say, "If you watch out and you duck, you may get out from underneath this."

This is a bigger problem than not just FOIA. The question is this: partnership with industry has got to be a real term not just a cliche. If they are co-partners in securing the homeland, we need to take into account what the statutory regulatory market looks like which completely predicts the notions of homeland security and ask whether or not public interest is being served through engaging in this activity. Sometimes they are going to come into conflict, and that's the role of government is to balance two public goods and reconcile them in a way that preserves our way of life.

What Jim is saying is absolutely right in that sense that by creating rules that basically protect and induce certain behavior, you are sending a signal to private industry that they are in fact co-partners in this project.

Chairman BOEHLERT. Thank you very much.

Ms. Jackson Lee.

Ms. JACKSON LEE. Thank you very much, Mr. Chairman. I think the panel represents an excellent representation of Federal and local participation, and I would offer to say that some of the insightful information is here just where it needs to be, in the local communities.

So let me thank you, first of all, for your presentations that have been brought forward, and let me acknowledge the fact that the legislation that we passed in the Science Committee has as one of its premises that we had no Federal agency that had the responsibility at that time of ensuring the Nation had a robust cyber security research enterprise. And I think that is one of the issues of this particular hearing to move that forward and to derive more information from that.

Let me also acknowledge, because we're in a particularly unique climate as we face July 4th and the resolve of this nation, that I'm so very proud of—and I acknowledge as a Member of the House Judiciary Committee any number of law enforcement agencies and first responders that were key to both the responding to September 11 but who have subsequently responded in a very forceful and effective way.

I think, Mr. Tritak, you have been enthusiastic or at least forthright in acknowledging Osama Bin Laden's existence but, as well, to say that he is not confined. He is not confined to the unusual creativity of September 11 that Americans could never imagine. We really should not shortchange him to limiting himself to physical areas; and, I think, that is a pronouncement that should be brought home locally because all of us are so intent on our Internet, so intent on our computer access, and it is extremely important.

With that backdrop of recognizing the broad breadth of terrorists and their mind set, I would hope that we will find private sector investors who will take up the challenge and will accept the fact that we have turned the page of American history and begin to focus on what they can do.

Let me add that I want to ensure as well, that we balance the Bill of Rights and our concern for that.

R&D FUNDS IN THE DEPARTMENT OF HOMELAND SECURITY (DHS)

I would simply pose this, Dr. Marburger, in this backdrop that I note you have said that we have $870 million in R&D. I would like to note how much of that amount that is budgeted will go into the proposed new Homeland Security Department. And, if you can, as I'm looking at the numbers, I find that the $870 million seems to be some 17 percent lower than our FY 2002, and we just got through speaking about the investment. I'd be interested in you responding to that distribution of funds and how we can increase that as we move forward.

Dr. MARBURGER. First of all, I do not have the figures of how much of this R&D money for cyber security would be represented in the pieces that will become part of the Department of Homeland Security. That information is not available at this point. It is only recently that we've identified all the pieces that would go in. But, for sure, some portion of it would be in the new office.

As far as the differences in requested—or in the annual budgets for this one year to the next, there's a table in Attachment B of my written testimony that gives some information about that.

It is important to make sure that the requests are appropriate, and one of the functions of my office is to coordinate agency requests to make sure that the requests are realistic and appropriate to the need. It is also necessary to get these requests through the appropriations committees and make sure that they come out.

I noted, for example, in the Department of Transportation, the enacted versus the request for FY '02 was disappointing. We need your help in getting attention to these things. I will work on my side to try to ensure that the requests are appropriate, and I will look forward to working with this committee and other committees in Congress to make sure that their follow-through is there, as well.

Ms. JACKSON LEE. Well, I will look forward to working with you in particular as we move through this process. It will be interesting to know if we can turn the corner in homeland security by adding additional funding to the Homeland Security Department. I think it's important to have those dollars and I would really like to see us not fall short of 2002. If it takes our efforts to do so, I certainly will join you enthusiastically on that.

AIR FORCE S&T BUDGET

I notice that the Air Force is looking to get $240 million. With respect to your input, Dr. Engle, would you share on how that will be helpful in what we're trying to do?

Dr. ENGLE. I can make more available to you for the record if you prefer.

Ms. JACKSON LEE. I will be happy to look at that.

Dr. ENGLE. Fundamentally our enterprise this year in S&T will amount to about $1.65 million. Of that, 10 percent is directly involved in the types of activities that this committee is interested in today. The additional roughly five or six percent that I mentioned in my total value for information investment goes largely to our command and control structure which, of course, is tightly interwoven to the protection of that transfer of information.

I don't want to mislead the Committee to think that we're investing that amount of money solely in cyber protection and cyber technology. A substantial portion of that amount is, but this also involved our work for building the air operation center for our war fighters, for the transfer of information in and out of that, for the work toward assurance, for the inventing and encrypting of information in novel ways for the transfer of information between actually different war fighting organizations but would also be useful for transfer of information security anywhere even in our commercial and industrial sectors of the United States. So an awful lot of work going into that particular area.

We have some substantial amount of work going into a part that probably the commercial sector shouldn't be interested in, and that is offensive cyber activities from the standpoint of what we do. And so there is an investment in that section, as well, which is probably unique to the military rather than to a broader Federal enterprise at this point in time.

And I can provide a full breakout of the specific funding of each of the various categories that we've earmarked, for you.

Chairman BOEHLERT. Thanks very much, Dr. Engle. That would be helpful for the Committee to have that breakdown. We'll share it with our colleagues.

Ms. JACKSON LEE. Thank you.

Chairman BOEHLERT. Thank you, Ms. Jackson Lee.

Chairman Smith.

Mr. SMITH. The success of the Al Qaeda, of the terrorists, of any terrorist, is partially going to be how much they disrupt us. They have done, I suspect, far more than they could have imagined already. We're spending billions of dollars in terms of the Federal Government's activities. In addition to that significant additional security from the airlines, from protecting our power grids, our source of generation. So anything that's transported, anything that uses energy, is going to cost more. So it reduces our competitive position a little bit.

I suspect in terms of the activities of the Federal Government, we're going to end up wasting a lot of talent, a lot of money, and so part of the question is, how far do we go in trying to protect ourselves?

And I don't know that there is anybody that can give that answer. As Chairman of the Basic Research Committee, I am convinced that additional research is probably not wasted; that the more we know about our systems probably, eventually the better able we will be to make those systems and our computer technology, our information technology more effective and more efficient.

But I am concerned about how far we go in terms of spending money because we are wasting a lot of energy that could be spent increasing our productivity, but what is actually happening is we're actually increasing the cost of everything we produce in this country; therefore, a little bit less competitive with our competitors that might be producing that product.

OPENNESS OF INFORMATION AND THE FOIA

Let me ask the question on the balance of being secretive. Already, Mr. Engle, there is no question that we've kept a lot more things classified saying they are secret when they don't need to be classified. This seems to be a potential time when we're going to make even more things secret of what government does and how they do it and where they're going with it.

So your reaction like in two areas—one, is the "balance" that Congressman Bartlett talked about. How much of our rights do we give up at a time when we're trying to protect ourselves?

And the other question is on the Freedom Of Information Act. The homeland security proposal by the President has some suggestion of tightening up the freedom of information so it's not all public. We have a policy in this country, but I would also like some reaction, maybe from all four of you to give your opinion on, is the fact that we publish—essentially all research that's done that uses Federal Government money is now published for the world to look at, see, evaluate, and, therefore, make somebody that wants to utilize that information in a way that will disadvantage us more readily available to them.

So, Dr. Marburger, I understand you're going to have to leave for a flight, so I'm going to start with you and then just briefly a reaction from the panel.

Dr. MARBURGER. Well, first of all, Congressman Smith, I don't completely agree with the zero sum character of openness and security. There are many things that we can do to increase the robustness and decrease the vulnerabilities of our system that are dual use, that will make them more valuable to us for economic competitiveness and so forth.

And I would hope that many of the expenditures that the private sector makes will not simply add to the cost of their products but actually make them more desirable and add to the value of them, and I do believe that technology can help us to be more sophisticated about the ways that we track things and identify things and protect ourselves against intrusions that will not decrease the liberties that we treasure so much in this country.

Certainly, it's President Bush's fondest hope that we will not diminish the quality of life for Americans as we protect ourselves in this war against terrorism. So the hope is that we can identify very narrowly the kinds of information that we need to protect; that we will not do anything foolish in helping our enemies; and that we bring all of the talent that we can to bear on this issue to establish an appropriate balance between openness and security.

So I believe that we are moving in the right directions. The provisions in the legislation for the Department of Homeland Security with respect to the FOIA legislation are fairly well defined. There is an effort to define national homeland security information that will address this issue. We're not just clamping down on all kinds of information but just on those kinds that we think will be of specific help to terrorists.

Mr. SMITH. Mr. Kallstrom.

Mr. KALLSTROM. Congressman Smith, I certainly agree with your premise and your concern, and I think we have a long track record of spending a lot of money on things that don't pay a lot of dividends, not through malice aforethought but through lack of communication, etcetera. We need to move on. We need to get out of the Cold War into the situation that faces us today, which is largely, I think, what John talked about.

It's a new time for us. It's a time of dependency on not just agencies like the FBI and the CIA as islands unto themselves, but it's a time of all of us working together.

I honestly believe that we can make a huge major impact on this issue of rounding up the scoundrels that are here if we could better equip state and local police with information, relevant, better information, real time, and at the same time take advantage of what the business side of the ledger has been using for decades and that is very sophisticated expert systems; that you write rules and it brings you, you know, through this high-pressure hydrant of information. Which when I was running the FBI office in New York City, my biggest challenge was dealing with that high pressure hydrant and trying to figure out, you know, what to act on.

In retrospect, it's clear what to act on when events happen. But when you don't have the ability to translate, you don't have the ability to actually hone down buckets and buckets of information. The private sector does this very, very conveniently and very, very efficiently.

I think we need some sort of a time out and let the private sector come into the Federal Government. You know, let the Tom Cybels of the world and others come in and redo these stovepipe databases that we have in the Federal Government that are not serving us well today as we face this challenge.

Mr. TRITAK. Congressman, I think what you are hitting on is a balancing act which doesn't lend itself to a very easy or simple answer. You know, if you look at what Al Qaeda is trying to do, as I told you before, in terms of the economy, they are not going to destroy the economy in any physical, material sense. We are much too robust. We are much too large.

The risk that it poses is a disengagement of economic behavior, a disengagement from our social institutions that is caused by a loss of confidence by the public at large in both our public and private institutions unless we take reasonable steps to safeguard and protect them. So we could very easily not lose productivity but an erosion in our very way of life, or the confidence that we are able to preserve our way of life in this new environment. I don't think anyone wants that. So the security paradigm is something we have to wrestle with.

On the other hand, we don't want to do Bin Laden's job for him. The fact of the matter is nothing would make him happier than for us to become oppressive, xenophobic and isolationist and to withdraw from the Middle East and the Persian Gulf and pull our culture back into our shores and stay away. My sense is if we do that, we probably would see the last of Bin Laden. We may see some other creep come along, but that's the other thing.

Finally, I want to say one thing about FOIA very quickly, because I also think—on one point you made earlier. You know, FOIA is just a tool. Okay. There's not going to be an avalanche of information sharing when we adjust these things, because the one thing FOIA can't do, except create a favorable environment, is you can't legislate or regulate trust.

And trust is, frankly, the essential ingredient to any collaborative, really good information sharing arrangement between government and industry. And that's going to take time.

I want to add one point that you made earlier that Jim touched on, which is, everyone is asking what is the Federal Government doing? Where is the strategy? Where are they going? Well, these are important questions that we're working on.

Do you want to know something? Don't wait for the Federal Government. You got a case for action in your hometown right now, and take that initiative. Just as Jim said, I got to tell you, sometimes the best stuff I've seen is people outside the beltway coming and saying, "Have you thought about this?" And the answer is "No."

The best minds of Washington aren't going to solve the homeland security problem within the beltway. It's going to be because State and local governments and private industry actually have taken on this case because they have a stake in homeland security and they are the targets also and come up with a model that actually goes from the bottom up. I know you'd like to work from bottom up as suggested here, maybe sideways.

Chairman BOEHLERT. Thank you very much for a very insightful commentary.

Dr. Engle.

Dr. ENGLE. Just briefly. Reflecting on your question, Congressman Smith, it occurs to me that our entire research effort—in fact, probably our entire enterprise in the United States Air Force, and I'd argue across government, is structured on a fundamental premise of openness in our society. We aren't doing research, quite frankly, to hide and/or protect or obfuscate, in any way, information, not in the direction we're going.

Quite the contrary. We're trying to develop systems that will allow us to communicate securely with those that require the information and to prevent the information flow to people who shouldn't have it. I mean that's translatable probably across our country, I would think. I mean I don't know. That's the fundamental nature of our freedom.

So, are we taking risks? Yes. Do I think we have too much risk in the way in which we protect and insure our information in our country today? Probably we do.

Can we stand that as a nation? I think we can. We have absorbed an immense amount of, I guess, leakage of our information to people that shouldn't have it, and so I don't know if balance is the right word or whether we're looking for the right mix of protection versus openness.

I would argue in your particular area of interest, basic research, I don't believe any of our research at that level is classified or protected in any way. It's completely open for all to see and to watch. As we get to very, very mature technology in the military and we're about to put in place something that could give our nation significant advantage or leverage against particular threats, then it tends to find its way into the classified domain. But, fundamentally, our research is an open forum. It has to be or it mitigates against our creativity and innovation.

So I can't specifically answer your question other than to say that I think that we are—our mix is right, and I hope that we don't probably slam the pendulum too far on the side of overprotection and hiding of information in our country.

Chairman BOEHLERT. Thank you very much, Dr. Engle.

Dr. Bartlett.

Mr. BARTLETT. Doctor, thank you very much.

PROTECTING THE NATION'S POWER AND COMMUNICATION GRIDS AGAINST A NUCLEAR ELECTROMAGNETIC PULSE (EMP)

Dr. Engle mentioned asymmetric threats, and Mr. Kallstrom mentioned the importance to our society and our economy of our power grids and communication grids and how much harm would be done if we lost those.

Let me ask you a question relevant to those two areas.

Before doing that, I would like to go back to a meeting that we had in Vienna, Austria. It was during the Kosovo conflict. There were 11 Members of Congress plus at least 10 other congressional witnesses to this and several staff members, and there were three members of the Russian Dumas there, and there was a personal representative of Slovodan Milosevic there.

One of the members of the Russia Dumas was Vladimir Lukin, who was Ambassador at the end of the Bush I and beginning of the Clinton Administrations. He was at that time chairman of their international relations or foreign affairs, whatever they call that committee in the Duma.

This is a statement that he made. He was very angry personally, by the way. He sat there for two days with his arms folded looking at the ceiling, and he said at one point, "Why should we help you?" "You spit on us and now why should we help you?"

We, by the way, developed the framework for ending the Kosovo conflict that was used by the G–8 five days later to, in fact, end that conflict.

But this was the statement that Vladimir Lukin made. Now, remember who he is. He said, "If we really wanted to hurt you with no fear of retaliation, we would launch an SLBM"—that comes from the ocean so you're uncertain from whom it came. "We would launch an SLBM. We would detonate a nuclear weapon high above your country and shut down your power grid and your communications for six months or so."

The third ranking Communist was one of the members of the Russia Dumas who was there. His name is Alexander Ashabanov. He smiled and said, "And if one weapon wouldn't do it, we have some spares. Like about 10,000."

Our first knowledge of this phenomenon called electromagnetic pulse came in 1962 at the Operation Starburst, I think it was. It was a detonation high over Johnston Island. It disrupted electrical and electronic activities 800 miles away in Hawaii. The Soviets, now the Russians, have a good deal more experience with that than us.

This is like a simultaneous lightening strike everywhere all at once with a rise time of nanoseconds so that none of the surge devices protect you from it.

We now have a commission, Title XIV of last year's Defense Authorization Act which sets up a commission chaired by Rumsfeld's deputy on his Commission on Ballistic Missile Threat, that's looking at the EMP threat.

What Mr. Lukin said was if it's launched from the ocean, you aren't going to be certain who launched it, and any way all they do is shut down our computers, which is what this does. Are we then justified in incinerating and vaporizing their babies and their grandmothers? That's going to be a tough call should that happen.

My question is, how are you preparing for this possibility; and how would we recover from it?

Dr. MARBURGER. I'm not sure I can answer that question very completely.

First of all, we have learned a lot since 1962. This is a kind of threat that's specifically understood by our military.

In my view, the use of nuclear weapons in any respect is an extreme eventuality but, nevertheless, one that we have to be prepared for. And I'm not qualified and I'm not prepared to speak to the Nation's nuclear strategy at this point. But, certainly, electromagnetic pulse is an extreme situation with respect to homeland security.

I think that we need to focus on the much larger number of threats that require much less technological capability of the enemy with respect to homeland security. This is a very sophisticated threat that could not be mounted by just every country.

So I think we should let our military representative on this panel speak on that.

[Laughter.]

Chairman BOEHLERT. Dr. Engle.

Dr. ENGLE. The characterization is correct. I mean the military had word of this problem for quite a long period of time.

Quite frankly, it's been focused on our nuclear response strategy, and so the technology that we have invested in over the years to ensure ourself some capacity to respond in a nuclear war is for a limited portion of our military assets, and I guess the message there is that we can survive that kind of attack. That technology is available.

Mr. BARTLETT. Excuse me. You mean militarily we can survive that kind of attack?

Dr. ENGLE. Certain parts of our military.

Mr. BARTLETT. We hope that we will be able to launch our intercontinental ballistic missiles to an EMP. That is not a certainty.

Dr. ENGLE. Well, not a certainty, but a very high probability that we would be able to do that.

Now, that doesn't say much for the rest of our conventional force structure. And I guess the thing that we worry mostly about right now is ruining our satellite infrastructure, commercial satellite infrastructure. Some of the military satellite infrastructure is hardened and secure.

Mr. BARTLETT. Two middle star satellites.

We would probably lose with one single high altitude burst $10 billion worth of satellites. It's the softest part of our infrastructure. All of those within line of sight we'd lose from prompt effects and the others would die quickly because the Van Allen belts are pumped up. And even if you'd launch a new satellite, it would survive for a very short period of time because of the pumped up Van Allen belts.

Dr. ENGLE. That's exactly correct.

And as a result, our research is focusing on a number of different areas. One is the mitigation of the pumped up Van Allen belt energy levels, and there is some very promising work at the basic research level at this point in time that portends that we can get to some solutions in that regard. And there is a significant amount of protection of systems that we're investing in at the same time, not just the United States Air Force but more pervasively.

From the standpoint of reconstitution nationally, in our national infrastructure, this is not necessarily problematic if we do the right kinds of things in industry to protect critical data and information because you can reconstitute it. I mean it doesn't take six months to reconstitute the ground-based infrastructure. It could take six months or longer to reconstitute the space-based, which is, again, probably one of our biggest focuses at this time.

Mr. BARTLETT. If this resulted in the loss of major transformers in our power grid, for those large ones there are none on the shelf and it takes 18 months to two years to get them.

In the attack on the Pentagon, we lost four transformers. We tried to patch two together from the parts of those four because with the priority of the Pentagon it's going to take six months to get those little transformers.

Most people do not know this, but there are no large transformers on the shelf. If you need one, they will build one for you.

Mr. TRITAK. If I may, Congressman. I think one thing we have learned from 9/11 is that the implausible is not impossible, and I think that is important to keep—I mean people you talked with before 9/11 and told them you could turn airplanes into cruise missiles, it would have been hard for some people to take. Okay.

And I also think the other important point is, is that the extent to which EMP could be created, the sort of thing you described also needs to be looked at. I'm not a scientist, so I can't say. But targeted use may also have its value in connection with broader effort that's being undertaken by a terrorist.

But let me just add one more final point. I think it's fine for our Russia colleagues to swagger the way they did in this meeting, and it sounds a bit like they were angry for other reasons. But the fact of the matter is for a level of recklessness on those actors of the kind that you would almost have to question their sanity because the entire strategy ultimately comes down to not being able to identify who did this, and that's a very high risk. And if you were willing to take those risks, why not just incinerate the United States while you're at it?

Because I will tell you, SAC and the rest of our nuclear force were built to deal with certain kinds of EMP threats, and if they caught something coming out of the ocean and they were able to identify within reasonable terms of its going and the next thing we know half our country is put out, the Russians better really be praying and built a level of capital in heaven because I think they would be in some serious trouble.

Chairman BOEHLERT. Thank you very much.

Ms. Jackson has a quick question of Dr. Marburger before he departs.

Ms. JACKSON LEE. And I appreciate very much the answer from some of the other members. But, very quickly, following up on Dr. Bartlett's comments about our satellites. We know we can deal with our home based cyber systems with maybe software improvement. But the satellite does pose a big problem, and here's an issue of collaboration.

Can NASA play a role? And what role would NASA play in helping us with the securing and/or research regarding our satellite systems?

Dr. MARBURGER. NASA does play a role in this type of research. And, in fact, immediately after the 1962 blast that Congressman Bartlett referred to, NASA went into a major program to find alternate sources of power generation for satellites and radiation damage studies. And in the intervening 40 years, it has been possible to make strides on this. NASA has been an important contributor and, of course, NASA sits on all the panels, the crosscutting coordination panels that share in the construction of our research program for cyber security.

Ms. JACKSON LEE. Although as the Chairman knows that I'm in the great State of New York, I come from Texas and we have great interest in the valuable work that NASA does. And so I wanted to make sure—and I hope, Dr. Marburger, if you take that message back that they can be valuable—they will also have the financial resources that might help them be even more successful in providing the support systems that are needed.

Let me conclude by posing this question and maybe others can answer if Dr. Marburger answers and leaves.

You did an assessment of the critical infrastructure areas that needed to be insured, if you will. Can you share with us some of the areas of vulnerabilities that we in the local community should be concerned about and should be looking to be helpful with?

Dr. MARBURGER. I wouldn't want to share too much detail about that. I think that the right response is to look at the obvious and that the systems of telecommunications and energy distribution, food distribution and bioterrorism—we haven't talked about bioterrorism at all today. Certainly the threat is always there. We had an incident of it last fall with the anthrax incident. And these are at the highest level types of concerns that we need to be addressing in these researches.

Even rural areas stand a lot to lose by a cyber terrorism incident. Denial of service and assets that are important to our daily lives could be disrupted by these attacks.

So I wouldn't want to be explicit about these, but there certainly are many opportunities for disrupting life in communities, such as this that we're meeting in today.

Chairman BOEHLERT. Thank you very much, Dr. Marburger. I know you have to depart. And I want to thank all the members of this panel, very valuable panel.

Your testimony will be supplemented by written submissions in response to some of the questions that were brought up during this panel. Dr. Marburger——

Dr. MARBURGER. Thank you very much.

Chairman BOEHLERT.—have a good trip back. And the others are excused.

We have one more panel and then we will be visiting the Air Force Research site and look forward to that.

Thank you very much.

[Whereupon, at 10:45 a.m., a recess was taken.]

Panel II

[Whereupon, at 10:55 a.m., the hearing was reconvened.]

Chairman BOEHLERT. I call this meeting back to order. We now have with us our second panel which I am pleased to introduce. The second panel consists of Mr. Robert Weaver, who is Deputy Special Agent-in-Charge of the New York Field Office and Director of the New York Electronic Crimes Task Force, with the United States Secret Service; Dr. Yacov Shamash, Dean of Engineering at the State University of New York at Stony Brook; and the third panelist is President and CEO of Dolphin Technologies, Inc., in Rome, New York, at the Technology Park, Mr. Michael Miravalle.

Gentlemen, thank you so much. We will go in the order introduced. First, Mr. Weaver, you're on.

STATEMENT OF MR. ROBERT WEAVER, DEPUTY SPECIAL AGENT-IN-CHARGE, NEW YORK FIELD OFFICE; DIRECTOR, NEW YORK ELECTRONIC CRIMES TASK FORCE, UNITED STATES SECRET SERVICE, NEW YORK, NEW YORK

Mr. WEAVER. Mr. Chairman, Congresswoman Jackson Lee, Congressman Smith and Congressman Bartlett. Thank you for allowing me to be part of this distinguished panel and the opportunity to address the Committee regarding computer security and how we can protect America's computer network from attack.

I offer this brief statement and ask that my entire statement be entered into the record.

Chairman BOEHLERT. Without objection, so ordered.

Mr. WEAVER. Thank you. And I agree with Ms. Jackson Lee, we can do this, and if I can offer some inspiration to the group, never give in and please never give up.

Mr. Chairman, let me once again thank you for your unwavering support on behalf of all the members of the task force. After the dark days of September 11, your commitment and dedication to our rebuilding efforts have been and remain to be inspirational to all of us who are committed to public service. The people of New York and in particular Upstate New York should be proud of the support and contributions coordinated by you and your office and this wonderful and powerful committee.

Yet another example from your guiding hand, the Committee's hand, is illustrated in the House Resolution 3394, Cyber Security Research and Development Act. That is good news for this country.

Two critical lessons learned from September 11 terrorist attack that destroyed the World Trade Center were leadership and communications. In the hours after the attack, the Secret Service, our New York field office and, more specifically, the New York Electronic Crimes Task Force immediately benefited from the decisive leadership you directed through the National Institute of Justice, the National Law Enforcement and Corrections Technology Center, the Cyber Center Laboratory located in Rome, New York, and the Office of Science and Technology.

If I may, please let the record show that you were the first to call and to offer support in terms of equipment, services, and technical assistance. We will always remember how you stood by our side to recover from this horrific attack and your continuing support in fighting the war on terrorism.

To commemorate the heroes of September 11 and to honor those who lost their lives, to include Secret Service Special Officer Craig Miller, and to recognize and honor the support and contributions of the citizens of Upstate New York, and with your permission, Mr. Chairman, we have chosen to display this battle worn flag, American flag, you see here today.

This flag was, as you pointed out, recovered from 7 World Trade Center and represents our patriotism to the United States and our continued commitment to our oath of office. I might add that this flag has never been displayed before today's public session and special occasion.

Mr. Chairman, the Secret Service fights cyber crime as part of its core mission to protect the integrity of our nation's financial payment systems. Since its inception, modes and methods of payment have evolved creating changes to our mission. Computers and other chip devices are now the facilitators of criminal activity or the targets of such. The perpetrators involved in the exploitation of such technology range from traditional fraud artists to violent criminals, all of whom recognize new opportunities and anonymous methods to expand and diversify their criminal portfolio.

During this era of change, one constant remains intact—our close working relationship with the banking and finance sectors as well as the telecommunications industry. Our history of cooperation with these industries is a result of our unique responsibilities in the protection of the integrity of our financial payment systems. The Secret Service has found a highly effective way to leverage these relationships in the battle against high tech crime through a model developed by our own New York Electronic Crimes Task Force.

While the Secret Service leads this innovative effort, we do not control nor dominate the participants or the investigative agenda of the task force. Rather, the task force impacts the community by providing a productive framework and collaborative crime fighting environment in which the resources of its participants can be combined to effectively and efficiently make a significant impact on electronic crimes.

Within the New York model, which was established in 1995, there are 50 different Federal, State and local law enforcement agencies represented as well as prosecutors, academic leaders, and over 200 different private sector corporations. We consider the New York model as the 21st Century law enforcement formula for success.

This innovative initiative further serves to enhance information sharing and to significantly increase the strength of our national Electronic Crimes Task Force initiatives which is based on this New York model. The PATRIOT Act directed the Secret Service to expand this model first to 18 cities across the United States, and the Service hopes to expand upon these further in the years to come.

I believe what separates this task force from all others and what truly gives us our unique brand that has generated so much success is our commitment and contribution to the community. Our core mission has always been simple: to make a difference, to have an impact on the community and to respond to the needs of our partners.

Mr. Chairman, law enforcement in general is not sufficiently equipped to train the masses nor can it compete with academic institutions. However, our partnership with industry and academia has demonstrated that this can be an integral part of the solution.

Partnerships are a very popular term in both government and private industry today, and everyone agrees there is great benefit to that approach. Unfortunately, and however, partnerships cannot be legislated, regulated or stipulated, nor can they be purchased, traded, or incorporated.

Partnerships are voluntarily built between people and organizations that recognize the value in joint collaboration toward a common end.

Let me relate the Secret Service mission in fighting cyber crime to the bigger picture of critical infrastructure protection. As previously stated, we target cyber crime as it may affect the integrity of our nation's financial payment and banking systems. In this context, our efforts to combat cyber assaults, which target information and communication systems, which in turn support the financial sector, are part of the larger and more comprehensive critical infrastructure protection scheme.

The whole notion of infrastructure protection embodies an assurance and confidence in the delivery of critical functions and services that in today's world are increasingly interdependent and interconnected. I've heard said that the good news is that the Internet is connected, and the bad news is that the Internet is connected.

To put this all in perspective, the public's confidence is lost if such delivery systems and services are unreliable or unpredictable, regardless of the cause of the problem. The Critical Systems Protection Initiative—we call it CSPI—a collaborative effort with Carnegie Mellon University, is a Secret Service initiative with the goal of establishing standards, guidelines and methodologies to incorporate a cyber security component to our traditional protection advances. It's uniqueness lies in the fact that it will not only consider the physical vulnerabilities as a venue for security requirements but also the forth dimension, the supporting information technology infrastructure of that venue.

An example of this was our successful implementation of a cyber security plan at the 2002 Winter Olympics and the 2002 Super Bowl in New Orleans, both designated "national special security events." Agents assigned to this role assisted their counterparts in preventing, investigating and managing numerous intrusion attempts and e-mail threats that took place during those major events.

A well-placed cyber attack against a weak technology or support infrastructure system can render an otherwise sound physical plan vulnerable and inadequate.

Mr. Chairman, it should also be noted that all deliberate infrastructure attacks, before they rise to such a threshold, are also cyber crimes and are likely to be dealt with initially by law enforcement personnel, both Federal, State and local, in the course of their routine business. In fact, I don't believe there is universal agreement as to when a hack or a network intrusion rises to the threshold of an infrastructure attack and corresponding national security event, but we would all probably recognize one when it reached catastrophic proportions.

Given this continuum and inter-play between computer-based crimes and national security issues, the Secret Service recognizes that its role in investigating computer-based attacks against the financial sector can be significant in the larger plan for the protection of our nation's critical infrastructures. When we arrest a criminal who has breached and disrupted sensitive communications and networks and are able to restore the normal operation of the host, be it a bank, a telecommunications carrier, or medical facility, we believe we've made a significant contribution toward assuring the reliability of the critical systems, and the public relies upon those on a daily basis.

Another important component in our investigative response to cyber crime is the Electronic Crimes Special Agent Program. This program is comprised of approximately 175 agents who have received extensive training in forensic identification, preservation, and retrieval of electronically stored evidence.

In spite of our limited resources, we do provide physical assistance on a regular basis to other departments for training or to perform computer-related analysis or technical consultation. In fact, so critical was the need for even basic training in this regard, the Secret Service joined forces with the International Association of Chiefs of Police and the National Institute of Justice to create the "Best Practices Guide" to searching and seizing electronic evidence, which is designed for the first responder, line officer or detective, alike.

We have also worked with this group to produce the interactive, computer-based training program known as "forward edge," a two CD package which takes the next step of training to conduct electronic crimes investigations in a virtual world. It incorporates the virtual reality features as it presents three different investigative scenarios to the trainee.

In today's high tech criminal environment, the challenge to Federal law enforcement and government is to identify existing repositories of expertise and provide a framework for inclusion and productive collaboration amongst the many government agencies and their respective industry and academic counterparts. The Secret Service is convinced that building these partnerships with the private sector and local law enforcement is the model for combating electronic crimes in this information age.

That concludes my prepared statement. I would be happy to answer your questions.

[The prepared statement of Mr. Weaver follows:]

PREPARED STATEMENT OF ROBERT WEAVER

Mr. Chairman, Members of the Committee, thank you for inviting me to be part of this distinguished panel, and the opportunity to address the Committee regarding computer security and how we can protect American computer networks from attack. Mr. Chairman, let me once again thank you for your unwavering support and advocacy on behalf of all of the members of our task force. After the dark day of September 11, 2001, your commitment and dedication to our rebuilding efforts have been and remains to be inspirational to all of us who are committed to public service. The people of New York and in particular upstate New York should be proud of the support and contributions coordinated by you and your office.

Two critical lessons learned from September 11, 2001 terrorist attack that destroyed the World Trade Center were leadership and communications. In the hours after the attack, the Secret Service, our New York Field Office, and more specifically, the New York Electronic Crime Task Force (NYECTF) immediately benefited from the decisive leadership you directed through, the National Institute of Justice (NIJ), the National Law Enforcement and Corrections Technology center, the Cyber Science Laboratory located at Rome, NY, and the Office of Science and Technology. If I may, please let the record show that you were the first to call and to offer support in terms of equipment, services, and technical assistance. We will always remember how you stood by our side to recover from this horrific attack and your continuing support in fighting the war on terrorism.

Comments and background regarding the battle-worn USA flag displayed

To commemorate the heroes of September 11th, to honor those who lost their lives, to recognize and honor the support and contribution of the citizens of upstate New York, and with the permission of Chairman Boehlert, we have chosen to display the battle worn American flag you see here today. This flag was recovered from the rubble of Number 7 World Trade Center and represents our patriotism to the United States and our continued commitment to our oath of office. I might add that this flag has never been displayed in public until today's special occasion.

The Secret Service fights cyber crime as part of its core mission to protect the integrity of this nation's financial payment systems. This role has evolved from our initial mandate to suppress the counterfeiting of currency upon our creation in 1865. Since this time, modes and methods of payment have evolved creating changes to our mission. Computers and other "chip" devices are now the facilitators of criminal activity or the target of such. The perpetrators involved in the exploitation of such technology range from traditional fraud artists to violent criminals—all of whom recognize new opportunities and anonymous methods to expand and diversify their criminal portfolio.

During this era of change, one constant remains intact: our close working relationships with the banking arid finance sectors as well as the telecommunications industry. Our history of cooperation with these industries is a result of our unique responsibilities in the protection of the integrity of our financial payments systems. We believe that protection of the banking and financial infrastructure and telecommunications is one of our "core competency" areas. As an agency, we seek to manage and apply our unique investigative and protective resources in the most efficient manner possible to the benefit of our telecommunications and financial institution partners.

Mr. Chairman, there is no shortage of information, testimony, or anecdotal evidence regarding the nature and variety of cyber-based threats to our telecommunications and banking and financial infrastructures and the need to create effective solutions. There is, however, a scarcity of information regarding successful models to combat such crime in today's high tech environment. This is where the Secret Service can make a significant contribution to current and future discussions of successful law enforcement efforts to combat cyber crime.

The Secret Service has found a highly effective formula for combating high tech crime a formula that has been successfully developed by our New York Electronic Crimes Task Force. While the Secret Service leads this innovative effort, we do not control nor dominate the participants or the investigative agenda of the task force. Rather, the task force impacts the community by providing a productive framework and collaborative crime-fighting environment in which the resources of its participants can be combined to effectively and efficiently make a significant impact on electronic crimes. Other law enforcement agencies bring additional criminal enforcement jurisdiction and resources to the task force while representatives from private industry, such as telecommunications providers, for instance, bring a wealth of technical expertise.

Within the New York model, which was established in 1995, there are 50 different Federal, State and local law enforcement agencies represented as well as prosecutors, academic leaders, and over 200 different private sector corporations. The wealth of expertise and resources that reside in this task force coupled with an unprecedented information sharing capability yields a highly mobile and responsive machine. In everyday task force investigations, local law enforcement officers hold supervisory positions while representatives from other agencies assume the role as the lead investigator in many of the complicated cross jurisdictional information system investigations. These investigations encompass a wide range of computer-based criminal activity, involving e-commerce frauds, intellectual property violations, telecommunications fraud, and a wide variety of computer intrusion crimes.

Since 1995, the task force has charged over 860 individuals with electronic crime losses exceeding $731 million. It has trained over 13,000 law enforcement personnel, prosecutors, and private industry representatives in the criminal abuses of technology. On the proactive side, the task force has identified tools and methodologies that can be employed by various partners to eliminate potential threats to their information systems. We consider the New York Electronic Crimes Task Force as the 21st century law enforcement model that incorporates partnerships and information sharing within its core competencies. This approach has been implemented successfully in various venues around the country. Recently established Electronic Crimes Task Forces (ECTFs) include: Boston, Washington, DC, Charlotte, NC, Chicago, Las Vegas, San Francisco, Los Angeles, and Miami, FL. These ECTFs will model, adopt the practices, and adapt themselves upon the proven successes of the NYECTF's established products, tools, services, deliverables, processes, and transfers that value-package to meet the needs of the community. Others will follow.

This initiative further serves to enhance information sharing and significantly increase the strength of the national ECTF initiatives and networks, based on the NYECTF model, which was directed through section 105 of the Patriot Act, enacted on October 26, 2001. In addition to providing law enforcement with the necessary technical training and resources, a great deal more can be accomplished in fighting cyber crime when these task forces harness and leverage our partnerships and resources that exist outside government in the private sector and academia.

The systemic approach of the task force is based on a business model. Its methodology is based on the principles of prevention, education, training and awareness, pre-incident response risk management, investigations, and prosecution. This systemic and holistic approach addresses the underlying issues of our cyber crime initiatives, "think globally, and act locally." This approach combines a business strategy and cultural change, producing a unique teamwork concept targeting risk management, best practices, due-diligence, pre-incident response planning, and enterprise protection planning. It is good business designed based on doing what is right for our country. This is a government success story, highlighted by unparalleled sharing of information, the ability to analyze data with our partners that is second to none, with a community-centric civil defense focus for protection of the homeland, and ultimately, our national security.

I believe what separates this task force from all others and what truly gives us our unique brand that has generated so much success, is our commitment to building trusted partnerships and placing the highest priority on that which is in the best interests of the community. It is this community, here in Utica and others like it, that benefit from its design.

Mr. Chairman, the greatest strength of the New York task force is our commitment and contribution to the community. Our core mission has always been simple—to make a difference, to have an impact on the community, and to respond to the needs of our law enforcement partners, consumers, and private industry. The community has always been and always will be our focus. This is the cornerstone of our strategic policy based on a foundation that focuses on: impact of the community, investigations, forensics, new technology, research and development, academia, and legislative initiatives.

Little did we know on that fateful day after the destruction of our office which destroyed many of our personal and professional records and mementos, that this community would stand by our side and help us to rebuild. Despite losing our building and our equipment, we realized, with your help, that we still had our most precious resource, each other. I cannot tell you how proud I am of not only the men and women of the Secret Service who work tirelessly on the task force day and night, but also the assistance and support of our task force partners that will never be able to be quantified. It was this support that allowed the task force to become operational within 48 hours of the attack and forced it to become a battle-tested, self-motivating army that is fighting back.

The most compelling testimony to the expertise and success of the NYECTF is the large number of regular requests received from local and foreign law enforcement agencies for either training or consultation in support of their own initiatives and programs. These requests have come from agencies all across the country, as well as foreign countries such as Australia, Ireland, Italy and Thailand. The Secret Service recognizes the need to promote international cooperation and remains proactive in the dissemination of information to law enforcement agencies, both domestically and internationally, regarding program initiatives and current telecommunications, financial and electronic crime trends. Mr. Chairman, we are committed to working closely with our law enforcement counterparts worldwide in response to cyber crime threats to commerce and financial payment systems. We currently have 18 offices in foreign countries and a permanent assignment at Interpol, as well as several overseas initiatives. Our foreign presence increases our ability to become involved in foreign investigations that are of significant strategic interest.

Law enforcement in general is not sufficiently equipped to train the masses nor can it compete with academic institutions of higher learning in the area of research and development. However, our partnerships with industry and academia have demonstrated that this can be an integral part of the solution. Partnerships are a very popular term in both government and the private industry these days and everyone agrees that there is great benefit in such an approach. Unfortunately, however, partnerships cannot be legislated, regulated, or stipulated. Nor can partnerships be purchased, traded or incorporated. Partnerships are voluntarily built between people and organizations that recognize the value in joint collaboration toward a common end. They are fragile entities, which need to be established and maintained by all participants and built upon a foundation of trust.

The Secret Service, by virtue of the protective mission for which we are so well known, has always emphasized discretion and trust in executing our protective duties. We learned long ago that our agency needed the full support and confidence of local law enforcement and certain key elements of the private sector to create and maintain a successful and comprehensive security plan. Furthermore, we are also keenly aware that we need to maintain a trusted relationship with our protectees so that we can work with them and their staffs to maintain the delicate balance between security and personal privacy. Everyone knows the Secret Service "protects and serves;" now, in the Information Age, our mission is to also "protect servers."

Our strength lies in our predisposition towards discretion and trust that naturally permeates our investigative mission where we enjoy quiet successes with our private sector partners. We have successfully investigated many significant cases with the help of our private sector partners such as network intrusions and compromises of critical information or operating systems. In such cases, even though we have technical expertise that is second to none, we still rely on our private sector counterparts to collaborate with us in identifying and preserving critical evidence to solve the case and bring the perpetrator to justice.

Equally important in such cases is conducting the investigation in a manner that avoids unnecessary disruption or adverse consequences to the victim or business. With the variety of operating platforms and proprietary operating systems in the private sector, we could not accomplish these objectives without the direct support of our corporate sector partners. In fact, in one recently completed complex investigation involving the compromise of a wireless communications earner's network, our case agent actually specified in the affidavit of the federal search warrant that representatives of the victim business be allowed to accompany federal agents in the search of the target residence to provide technical assistance. This is unprecedented in the law enforcement arena and underscores the level of trust we enjoy with those we have built relationships with in the private sector. It is also indicative of the complexity of many of these investigations and serves to highlight the fact that we in law enforcement must work with private industry to be an effective crime fighting force. In approving this search warrant, the court recognized that in certain cases involving extraordinarily complex systems and networks, such additional technical expertise could be a critical, and sometimes imperative, component of our investigative efforts.

Let me relate the Secret Service's mission in fighting cyber crime to the bigger picture of critical infrastructure protection. As previously stated, we target cyber crime as it may affect the integrity of our nation's financial payment and banking systems. As we all know, the banking and finance sector comprises a very critical infrastructure sector and one which we have historically protected and will continue to protect. In this context, our efforts to combat cyber assaults, which target information and communication systems, which in turn support the financial sector, are part of the larger and more comprehensive critical infrastructure protection scheme. The whole notion of infrastructure protection embodies an assurance and confidence in the delivery of critical functions and services that in today's world are increasingly interdependent and interconnected. To put this all in perspective, the public's confidence is lost if such delivery systems and services are unreliable or unpredictable, regardless of the cause of the problem.

Regarding information security, the Secret Service has focused its efforts within a relatively narrow spectrum defined by its jurisdictional authorities and our financial payment systems. In this respect the Secret Service electronic crimes task force initiative has played, and will continue to play, an increasingly critical role.

The Critical Systems Protection Initiative (CSPI), a collaborative effort with Carnegie Mellon University, is a Secret Service initiative with the goal of establishing standards, guidelines and methodologies to incorporate a "cyber security" component to our traditional protection advance. Its uniqueness lies in the fact that it will not only consider the physical vulnerabilities of a venue for security requirements but also the fourth dimension, the supporting information technology infrastructure (i.e., information systems interdependencies amongst automated systems, wireless vulnerabilities, etc.).

An example of this is the implementation of a cyber security plan at the 2002 Winter Olympics and the 2002 Super Bowl in New Orleans, Louisiana. Agents assigned to this role assisted their counterparts in preventing, investigating and managing numerous intrusion attempts and e-mail threats.

We also recognize that our unique protective responsibilities, including our duties as the lead federal agency for coordinating security, at National Special Security Events, demand heightened electronic security awareness and preparation. A well-placed cyber attack against a weak technology or support infrastructure system can render an otherwise sound physical security plan vulnerable and inadequate.

Mr. Chairman, it should also be noted that all deliberate infrastructure attacks, before they rise to such a threshold, are also cyber crimes and are likely to be dealt with initially by law enforcement personnel, both Federal and local, in the course of routine business. In fact, I don't believe there is universal agreement as to when a "hack" or network intrusion rises to the threshold of an infrastructure attack and corresponding national security event but we would all probably recognize one when it reached catastrophic proportions.

Given this continuum and interplay between computer-based crimes and national security issues, the Secret Service recognizes that its role in investigating computer-based attacks against the financial sector can be significant in the larger plan for the protection of our nation's critical infrastructures. When we arrest a criminal who has breached and disrupted a sensitive communications network and are able to restore the normal operation of the host—be it a bank, telecommunications carrier, or medical service provider—we believe we have made a significant contribution towards assuring the reliability of the critical systems that the public relies upon on a daily basis.

As a footnote, the New York task force meets regularly with representatives from Wall Street and the Financial Services Information Sharing and Analysis Center (FS/ISAC) that was created pursuant to Presidential Decision Directive (PDD) 63. The directive mandated the Department of the Treasury to work with members of the banking and finance sector to enhance the security of the sector's information systems and other infrastructures, a responsibility managed by Treasury's Assistant Secretary of Financial Institutions. The role of the FS/ISAC is to devise a way to share information within the financial services industry relating to cyber threats and vulnerabilities. The Secret Service feels that it can make a significant contribution to the work of the FS/ISAC and is exploring common areas of interest with the FS/ISAC, to include information sharing, information technology, and expertise in technical, physical security and administrative areas of concern.

The Secret Service is also continuing to receive requests from local law enforcement agencies and others for assistance, and we welcome those requests. On an alarmingly increasing basis, our local field offices and the Financial Crimes Division of the Secret Service receive desperate pleas from local police departments for physical assistance, training and equipment in the area of computer forensics and electronic crimes so that they can continue to provide a professional level of service and protection for their citizens. In short, the Secret Service has become another option for local law enforcement, the private sector and others to turn to when confronted with network intrusions and other sophisticated electronic crimes.

An important component in our investigative response to cyber crime is the Electronic Crimes Special Agent Program (ECSAP). This program is comprised of approximately 175 special agents who have received extensive training in the forensic identification, preservation, and retrieval of electronically stored evidence. Special Agents entering the program receive specialized training in all areas of electronic crimes, with particular emphasis on computer intrusions and forensics. ECSAP agents are computer investigative specialists, qualified to conduct examinations on all types of electronic evidence, including computers, personal data assistants, telecommunications devices, electronic organizers, scanners and other electronic paraphernalia. It is in this very program that the Secret Service, as an agency of the Federal Government, has identified the state of affairs in security information and training. The Secret Service has leveraged funding to local and State law enforcement to train and equip local and State members of the NYECTF with the same training and tools as its own agents. This is an area that the Federal Government should exercise greater latitude in funding such programs for other than federal agencies. The need for consistency and education in this area should be expanded.

Since 2000, Secret Service trained ECSAP agents have completed over 3,463 examinations on computer and telecommunications equipment. Although the Secret Service did not track the number of exams done for other law enforcement agencies during this period, it is estimated that some 10 to 15 percent of these examinations fell in this category. Many of the examinations were conducted in support of other agencies' investigations such as those involving child pornography or homicide cases simply because the requesting agency did not have the resources to complete the examination itself.

In spite of our limited resources, we do provide physical assistance on a regular basis to other departments, often sending ECSAP agents overnight to the requesting venue to perform computer related analyses or technical consultation. In fact, so critical was the need for even basic training in this regard that the Secret Service joined forces with the International Association of Chiefs of Police and the National Institute for Justice to create the "Best Practices Guide to Searching and Seizing Electronic Evidence" which is designed for the first responder, line officer and detective alike.

We have also worked with this group to produce the interactive, computer-based training program known as "Forward Edge" which takes the next step in training officers to conduct electronic crime investigations. Forward Edge incorporates virtual reality features as it presents three different investigative scenarios to the trainee. It also provides investigative options and technical support to develop the case. Copies of state computer crime laws for each of the fifty states as well as corresponding sample affidavits are also part of the two-CD training program and are immediately accessible for instant implementation.

Thus far we have dispensed over 300,000 "Best Practices Guides" to local and Federal law enforcement officers and we are in the process of distributing, free of charge, over 20,000 Forward Edge training CDs.

The sharing of information has long been a pillar of the Secret Service institutional culture. The Secret Service believes firmly that the timely exchange of critical information is a vital component to the successful execution of our mission. Demonstrative of this belief is the Service's extensive use of "detailees" to other agencies with interests and missions of mutual interest.

Some examples of these are current detailees to:

- FinCEN
- Federal Trade Commission (Identity Theft)
- Operation Green Quest
- National Infrastructure Protection Center (NIPC).

These detailees serve the vital role of ensuring that information of mutual interest is quickly and accurately relayed from one entity to the other. Additionally, these detailees effectively expand the capacities of the affected agencies by enlisting the support and resources of the partner agency.

In an additional effort to further enhance information sharing between the law enforcement community and the financial industry, the Secret Service recently created the "E Library" Internet website which serves as a mechanism for all members to post specific information, images and alerts relating to fictitious financial instruments, counterfeit checks, and credit card skimming devices. This website is accessible free of charge to all members of the law enforcement and banking communities and is the only such tool of its kind.

In today's high tech criminal environment, the challenge to Federal law enforcement and government is to identify existing repositories of expertise and provide a framework for inclusion and productive collaboration amongst the many government agencies and their respective industry and academic counterparts. The Secret Service is convinced that building trusted partnerships with the private sector and local law enforcement is the model for combating electronic crimes in the Information Age.

Mr. Chairman, that concludes my prepared statement, and I would be happy to answer any questions that you or other Members of the Subcommittee may have.

Biography for Robert Weaver

Robert Weaver has served in government for nearly 25 years and in the Secret Service for nearly 20 years. He currently holds the position of Deputy Special Agent-in-Charge of the New York Field Office, and also serves as the head of the New York Electronic Crimes Task Force. As part of his duties, he is responsible for coordinating and supporting a wide range of financial crime investigations—including critical infrastructure protection, various forms of electronic crimes, credit card fraud, identity theft and telecommunications fraud—as well as training our law enforcement and private industry partners in the criminal abuses of technology and how to prevent them.

Weaver began his career with the Secret Service in 1982 as a Special Agent assigned to the Washington Field Office, and since that time has served in a variety of positions, including Team Leader of the Secret Service's Counter Assault Team and a tour of duty with the Vice Presidential Protective Division.

Prior to joining the Secret Service, Weaver earned his undergraduate degree from Central Connecticut State University and subsequently served with the Federal Bureau of Investigation and as an assistant to Supreme Court Justice Warren Burger. After joining the Secret Service, he earned a Master's of Forensic Science from George Washington University. Today, as head of the New York Electronic Crimes Task Force, he supervises a dedicated staff of high tech crime fighters and criminal investigators who are respected throughout law enforcement, the private sector, and academia. Respected both within the Secret Service, by members of the business community, and other law enforcement agencies, Weaver brings a down-to-earth perspective to the complex world of criminal abuse of technology.

Chairman BOEHLERT. Thank you very much, Agent Weaver.

Dr. Shamash.

STATEMENT OF DR. YACOV SHAMASH, DEAN OF ENGINEERING, STATE UNIVERSITY OF NEW YORK AT STONY BROOK, STONY BROOK, NEW YORK

Dr. SHAMASH. Mr. Chairman, distinguished Members and guests. Thank you for giving me the opportunity to speak to you today about how we can work together as New Yorkers and as Americans to successfully combat one of the most critical problems our state and our nation faces in the post 9/11 world.

I would like to tell you about the unsurpassed resources of New York State's outstanding research, higher education and information technology industry sectors and how we can bring them together to address these very serious matters.

Since 9/11, I have been working on these issues with colleagues not only in our institution, at Brookhaven National Labs and in local industry but also across the SUNY system, as chair of SUNY's Homeland Defense Infrastructure Task Force created by Chancellor King last fall.

These experiences have convinced me that our state is uniquely positioned. While addressing a problem of this magnitude would necessarily involve resources and institutions from around the Nation, I believe strongly that a focused national effort in cyber security could find no better home base than New York. And in my testimony today, I would like to tell you why.

But first, I would like to recognize Chairman Boehlert and the Members of the Science Committee for their vision and leadership in initiating the Cyber Security Research and Development Act. What is striking about this bill is not only the fundamental importance of its goal, protecting our nation against cyber terrorism, but also its deep understanding of how research and development and technology transfer are done.

H.R. 3394 wisely addresses the education and training aspect of cyber security, with its grants for 4-year and 2-year college programs as well as post-doc's and the R&D aspect through its cyber security research centers and NIST-based industry-academic and senior scientist programs. I hope your colleagues in the Senate will follow the trail you have blazed.

A little bit about my background. Over the last 20 years, I have devoted much of my energy to organizing and developing programs and entities in which industry, research and higher education come together to pursue discovery, to disseminate new knowledge and to develop new products.

I would like to share with you, briefly, some of those experiences, whether it's the establishment of an NSF industry/university department research center or the establishment of two NSF material science and research centers, whether it's establishing two centers for advanced technology in our state. And, more recently, I have been very much involved with the Governor's visionary plan to establish centers of excellence around the state, and I'm leading the efforts at Stony Brook in the area of center of excellence in the wireless Internet. That center in itself is a partnership between industry and academia and State government with an investment of $50 million by the state and $150 million by industry.

Again, we're looking at partnerships, and I think partnerships is going to be our secret weapon in this fight.

What is a cyber attack? Solving a problem always starts with defining the problem. As we have seen, fire walls can be very effective in shielding at the periphery—protecting server applications that do not have to be accessible to the Internet. And cryptography—encryption of communications—has basically solved the problem of communication security while the information is in transit.

The more serious problem has to do with system security. What happens when the information takes off the off ramp from the information super highway and enters and circulates within a local system, as is shown by the recent increase in computer virus and worm problems? However, even though malicious attacks cost companies almost $15 billion to clean up in 2001, viruses created by hackers and computer nerds for their private entertainment are only part of the system security puzzle.

The far more serious threat looming on the horizon is that of comprehensive, coordinated attacks by skilled cyber terrorists. Using mobile code or subverting trusted code, cyber attackers could bypass fire walls, obtain, observe or modify confidential or even classified information in transmission or systems or user files. Attackers can saturate their targets, Internet links, cause denial of service on critical or heavily used web sites, continuously monitor traffic and its contents to identify special vulnerabilities or discover threats to themselves or even establish a Trojan horse base inside our homeland for future attacks.

The fact that cyber security spending has increased tenfold over the last decade while the reported incidence of cyber attacks has increased by a factor of 120 indicates that existing cyber security solutions are not very effective. Currently available defense strategies tend to be after the fact. Attempts to respond in real time are hindered by the speed in which attackers can enter and leave a system as compared with the relatively longer time it takes for intrusion-detection systems to perform.

The Committee has really gotten it right in designing an R&D program that provides incentives for academic researchers with their longtime skills and deep interest in advancing basic knowledge to collaborate with industrial software developers, with their product orientation and their on-time/on-budget value structure. I believe that getting the most out of the investment you propose requires a comprehensive approach combining research, industry outreach, and training.

Now, why in New York? New York stands out among all the states of the United States in terms of its vulnerability to cyber attack—as the world's financial center, the world's media and communications center and a major center of world trade, the failure of critical business and communication systems in our state would have implications of extraordinary and perhaps permanent magnitude for us, for the Nation and, indeed, for the world.

The unprecedented shutdown of New York stock exchanges last fall offered a brief glimpse of what could happen if we do not act now to protect these critical systems. Fortunately, New York also stands out for the intellectual resources that it can mobilize to take up the many daunting challenges involved in successfully securing these systems. New York State has a critical mass of resources in cyber security that spans academic institutions, the public and private sectors and government.

The academic resources of New York State for cyber security are commanding. As we heard earlier, there are actually five centers, national security agency centers for academic excellence and information assurance, here in the State of New York: one at Buffalo, one at Stony Brook, one is at West Point, one at Syracuse and one is at Polytechnic. New York has two of the twelve DOD Critical Infrastructure Protection and Information Assurance Fellow Awards that were made this past year, one at Stony Brook and the other at Cornell.

The world class caliber of research in the state has been underscored by Governor Pataki's vision in funding centers of excellence throughout the state. In addition to Stony Brook, there is one at Buffalo, one in Albany, Rochester and Syracuse.

And New York is most fortunate to have two Federal research labs. Rome Lab's distinguished history of leadership in the information systems that underlie our nation's critical command and control apparatus and its current center role in the information directorate of the Air Force research lab, makes it a natural key player in this initiative; with additional IC IT institutions including the institution that we're at today, Syracuse, the SUNY campuses in the area and across the state, the Utica-Rome region is clearly an important geographic focus; Brookhaven National Laboratory which is managed by Stony Brook together with Battelle Memorial Institute.

New York State is equally fortunate in the superb cyber resources of its technology industry sector. I will just mention a few—IBM, Reuters, Computer Associates.

We should recall that New York was able to respond to and recover from the attacks of September 11 because of the tremendous resources of the city, state and local agencies. To benchmark the scale of what the City had to respond to that day according to Con Edison, the World Trade Center complex alone drew the same amount of power as the entire city of Albany, New York. Nowhere else will you find the infrastructure on the same scale that you find in New York State.

How can we get there from here? How would a national cyber security center be organized to fulfill its critical mission? Let's start with a mission statement.

The mission of a national center for cyber security is to mobilize our state's and our nation's best academic, research and industry resources to define the critical threats to our national information infrastructure, to develop the most effective solutions through both new countermeasures and strengthened systems, and to disseminate those solutions and the expertise to implement them.

Our campus experience with the NSF centers and the management of Brookhaven National Labs, which we did through the research foundation of SUNY in partnership with Battelle, gives us some idea of how to go about establishing a partnership here in the State of New York that can capitalize on the establishment of this center.

To achieve the goals of collaborative industry-university research and development, tech transfer and education and training, a national center should be administered through an organization that joins together the best resources of multiple institutions and industry partners to ensure that the brightest and most knowledgeable minds are engaged by the critical problems and to achieve the best solutions.

Now, that transfer is extremely important, and I think we have a lot of experience. I will not go through that, Mr. Chairman. I think you have that in my statement.

But I do want to mention one thing: At Stony Brook University, we have some incubators. We have 21 companies in our incubators that are growing, that are maturing. Taking the technology and actually implementing it in practice and getting it to the market is extremely important. I think that is an important aspect of any center that we establish. We must have an incubator, also, to go with it.

In closing, I would like to congratulate the Committee on its vision and its leadership in driving forward this vital—this critical cyber security initiative. You have determined an absolutely fundamental need for our national defense and have created a superb opportunity for New York's and our nation's leading edge academic and industrial researchers to act immediately to conduct the necessary research for new cyber security strategies and technologies—where our nation and our state, especially the industries that are such an important part of our state economy, need them so urgently.

Thank you, Mr. Chairman.

Chairman BOEHLERT. Thank you very much.

[The prepared statement of Dr. Shamash follows:]

PREPARED STATEMENT OF YACOV SHAMASH

Securing Our Nation's Information Infrastructure: New York Has What IT Takes

Introduction

Mr. Chairman, distinguished Members and guests: Thank you for giving me the opportunity to speak to you today about how we can work together as New Yorkers and as Americans to successfully combat one of the most critical problems our state and our nation faces in the post-9/11 world. I am Yacov Shamash from the State University of New York at Stony Brook and I would like to tell you about the unsurpassed resources of New York State's outstanding research, higher education and information technology industry sectors and how we can bring them together to address these very serious matters.

I serve as Dean of the College of Engineering and Applied Sciences and Vice President for Economic Development at Stony Brook—the latter a position almost unique in American higher education, which was created to enhance the impressive success we have achieved in developing industry-University partnerships. Since 9/11, I have been working on these issues with colleagues not only in our institution, at Brookhaven National Laboratory and in local industry, but also across the SUNY system, as Chair of SUNY's Homeland Defense Infrastructure Task Force. These experiences have convinced me that our state is uniquely positioned. New York can make a historic contribution to our national information security posture while also, in the spirit of self-reliance, developing means and mechanisms to protect ourselves and the New York-based financial services, telecommunications and other industries that are so important to the national and global economies. While addressing a problem of this magnitude would necessarily involve resources and institutions from around the nation, I believe strongly that a focused national effort in cyber security could find no better home base than New York and in my testimony today I would like to tell you why.

First, however, I would like to recognize the Chair, Congressman Boehlert, the Ranking Member, Congressman Hall, and the Members of the Science Committee—New Yorkers know Congressman Grucci well as a good friend of science and technology—for their vision and leadership in initiating the Cyber Security Research and Development Act. What is striking about this bill is not only the fundamental importance of its goal, protecting our nation against cyber terrorism, but also its deep understanding of how research and development and technology transfer are done. H.R. 3394 wisely addresses the education and training aspect of cyber security, with its grants for four-year and two-year college programs as well as postdocs, and the R&D aspect through its cyber security research centers and NIST-based industry-academic and senior scientist programs. I hope your colleagues in the Senate will follow the trail you have blazed.

Let me give you a little background information so that you can judge my credibility for yourselves. For the last twenty years, I have devoted much of my energy to organizing and developing programs and entities in which industry, research and higher education come together to pursue discovery, to disseminate new knowledge, in both the student body and the workforce, and to develop new products and get them out the door and into the marketplace where they improve and enrich and defend our lives. I would like to share with you briefly some of the experiences that I believe can help guide the creation of dynamically successful cyber security centers for our state's and our nation's preservation.

Cooperative Industry-University Research Center in Analog-Digital Circuits. At Washington State University I was fortunate to lead a team that won designation from the National Science Foundation as the state's first Cooperative Industry-University Research Center, which achieved its mission of attracting industry market leaders who were fierce competitors in the marketplace and engage them with university faculty in collaborative "pre-competitive" research in order to advance the state of the art in micro-electronics and ensure that our nation's technology industries continued to remain at the forefront in what continues to be a critical technology sector.

Strategic Partnership for Industrial Resurgence (SPIR). Seven years ago I encouraged my colleagues, the deans of SUNY's other engineering colleges, to work with State Senator LaValle and his colleagues to create the SPIR program, whereby advanced technology assistance across the engineering and technology disciplines is provided to New York companies, whether their needs are immediate manufacturing process assistance or long-term new product development. With a total cumulative State investment of less than $6 million during the life of the program, SPIR has helped more than 200 participating New York State companies perform more than 950 projects creating or saving a cumulative projected total of more than 8,000 jobs and bringing more than $70 million in non-State funds to New York.

I am proud that the College of Engineering has made Stony Brook the only university in the Nation with two NSF Materials Research Science and Engineering Centers. University scientists work in these centers side by side with industry scientists to develop new materials solutions for technology problems in the areas of polymers and thermal spray technology. Both of these centers work at the frontiers of their respective technologies but both also have a range of industry partners from high tech to "low tech." The College also competed successfully in New York's Center for Advanced Technology program: Stony Brook is the only campus with two CATS. Both have substantial industry clienteles, and the biotechnology center is recognized for its State-leading economic impact activities. In the last two years, I was asked by the University to lead our successful efforts to win designation as a STAR Center (Strategically Targeted Academic Research Center) in Biomolecular Diagnostics and Therapeutics and as New York State's Center of Excellence in the Wireless Internet and Information Technology. These centers, which will conduct R&D under industry-driven, industry-cosponsored programs, won a combined state award of almost $70 million to enhance the university's R&D infrastructure. With more than $115 million in industry matching funds, the Center of Excellence represents a $200 million program in information technology.

What is a cyber attack? Solving a problem always starts with defining the problem. As we have seen, firewalls can be very effective in shielding at the periphery—protecting server applications that do not have to be accessible to the Internet. And cryptography—encryption of communications—has basically solved the problem of communications security *while the information is in transit.* The more serious problem, as we are beginning to realize, has to do with *system* security—what happens when the information takes the off-ramp from the information superhighway and enters and circulates within a local system—as is shown by the recent increase in computer virus and worm problems However, even though malicious attacks cost companies almost $15 *billion* to clean up in 2001, viruses created by "hackers" and computer nerds for their private entertainment are only part of the system security puzzle. The far more serious threat looming on the horizon is that of comprehensive, coordinated attacks by skilled cyber terrorists. Using mobile code or subverting trusted code, cyber attackers could bypass firewalls, obtain, observe or modify confidential or even classified information in transmissions or system or user files. Attackers can saturate their targets' Internet links, cause denial-of-service on critical or heavily used websites, continuously monitor traffic and its contents to identify special vulnerabilities or discover threats to themselves, or even establish a "Trojan horse" base inside our homeland for future attacks.

Everyone in this room can envision the chaos that a well-coordinated cyber attack could cause. The potential costs are almost incalculable, but they include disabling our financial, trading, telecommunications, transportation, and/or power generation and transmission systems—any one of which could have severe and lasting economic as well as immediate material consequences.

The fact that cyber security spending has increased tenfold over the last decade, while the reported incidence of cyber attacks has increased by a factor of 120 indicates that existing cyber security solutions are not very effective. Currently available defense strategies tend to be "after-the-fact;" attempts to respond in real time are hindered by the speed with which attackers can enter and leave a system, as compared with the relatively longer time it takes for intrusion detection systems to perform. The youth and competitiveness of the software industry has focused software development on functionality and features, rather than security and reliability; cyber security is not an arena where the structure of the marketplace has attracted the private sector. The Committee has really gotten it right in designing an R&D program that provides incentives for academic researchers, with their long timescales and deep interest in advancing basic knowledge, to collaborate with industrial software developers, with their product orientation and their on-time/on-budget value structure. I believe that getting the most out of the investment you propose requires a comprehensive approach combining three elements:

- Both basic and applied research into new paradigms and approaches for protecting systems and detecting attacks, especially conducted with industry
- Technology transfer and industry outreach

- Education and training for both end users and system administrators and information technology officers

A successful national cyber security center will provide a centralized forum for directing the best efforts at all three of these elements.

Why New York? New York stands out among all the states of the United States in terms of its vulnerability to cyber attack—as the world's financial center, the world's media and communications center and a major center of world trade, the failure of critical business and communication systems in our State would have implications of extraordinary and perhaps permanent magnitude for us, for the Nation and indeed for the world. The unprecedented shutdown of the New York Stock Exchange last fall offered a brief glimpse of what could happen if we do not act now to protect these critical systems. Fortunately, New York also stands out for the intellectual resources that it can mobilize to take up the many daunting challenges involved in successfully securing these systems. We have one of the best public university systems in the nation, numerous fine private colleges and universities that also have the relevant expertise, federal laboratories, one of our nation's public military academies, and some of the largest cyber security companies in the country. New York State has a critical mass of resources in cyber security that spans academic institutions, the public and private sectors, and government.

The academic resources of New York State for cyber security are commanding. Two of SUNY's four university centers are home to NSA (National Security Agency) Centers for Academic Excellence in Information Assurance Education (IAE), Stony Brook and Buffalo; Stony Brook's Department of Computer Science consistently ranks in the top 15 in national quality assessments. In addition, SUNY has a wealth of four- and two-year colleges and specialized schools, such as the College of Technology at Utica-Rome, to address the workforce education needs of a major effort in cyber security throughout New York State. Such private institutions as Columbia, Cornell, Rensselaer, and New York University also have highly distinguished computer science programs, and Polytechnic and Syracuse also have NSA IAE centers. New York has two of the twelve DOD Critical Infrastructure Protection and Information Assurance Fellow (CIPIAF) awards made this past year, one at Stony Brook and the other at Cornell. Stony Brook has created a Center for Cyber Security, which includes a Secure Systems Lab, to consolidate its efforts in this fundamental area.

The world-class caliber of research in the state has been underscored by Governor Pataki's vision in funding Centers of Excellence throughout the state to support major technology development with industry partners. In addition to Stony Brook's center for which the Governor has committed $50 million in State funds, other centers are to be located at Buffalo, Albany, Rochester, and Syracuse.

New York is fortunate in being home to two important Federal research laboratories. Rome Lab's distinguished history of leadership in the information systems that underlie our nation's critical command and control apparatus, and its current central role in the information directorate of the Air Force research laboratory, makes it a natural key partner in this initiative. Brookhaven National Laboratory, located on Long Island and one of the few national laboratories that is managed by a university—Stony Brook, together with the Battelle Memorial Institute—recently helped make New York the recipient of three of the six recently awarded Federal NanoCenters which will spearhead development of these essential new technologies.

New York State is equally fortunate in the superb cyber resources of its technology industry sector, which is comprised of Fortune 500 companies as well as small entrepreneurial ventures. We need only to touch on the capabilities of such giants as IBM, Computer Associates—which continues to develop its comprehensive "best-of-breed" online security suite, eTrust—and Reuters Information Technologies, which delivers highly sensitive, mission-critical financial information daily in real time to its hundreds of thousands of customers around the world. In the months and years ahead, we will be greatly increasing our familiarity with the thousands of small software companies and start-ups that are contributing to the vitality of this sector across the State. Long Island alone is home to over a thousand of them, represented by their industry trade association, the Long Island Software and Technology Network (LISTnet). In developing industry partnerships for the Center of Excellence in the Wireless Internet and Information Technology at Stony Brook, we have been impressed to learn about the great variety of capabilities these companies have that are already being used and can be deployed to strengthen our information infrastructure and to improve security in other arenas.

We should recall that New York was able to respond to and recover from the attacks of September 11 because of the tremendous resources of the City, state, and local agencies. Other government agencies throughout the country have used New

York as a model to assess their preparedness in the event of other terrorist attacks. To benchmark the scale of what the City had to respond to that day: according to Con Edison, the World Trade Center Complex alone drew the same amount of power as the entire city of Albany, NY. Nowhere else will you find infrastructure on the same scale as New York.

How can we get there from here; how would a national cyber security center be organized to fulfill its critical mission? Let's start with a mission statement: the mission of a national center for cyber security is to mobilize our state's and our nation's best academic, research and industry resources to define the critical threats to our national information infrastructure, to develop the most effective solutions, through both new countermeasures and strengthened systems, and to disseminate those solutions and the expertise to implement them as well as to be constantly on the alert for ways to identify new threats. While the mission is new, the means to fulfill it can borrow effectively from responses our society has developed to other national "grand challenges" that have been described by our nation's science, engineering and policy leadership in recent years. Our campus' experience with the NSF MRSEC program and the New York State CAT program shows how successfully those responses can be organized through focused R&D programs partnering industry and academia and involving multiple institutions with multiple participants at multiple sites, under the guidance of a steering committee on which each of the major academic and industry contributors is represented. Under the circumstances, the overall priority set for the research program would probably be dictated by the new Office of Homeland Security with specific research projects to be recommended by an advisory board reporting to the steering committee and comprised of representatives from industry, major research organizations and government entities.

To achieve the goals of collaborative industry-university research and development, technology transfer and education and training, a national center should be administered through one institution but should join together the best resources of multiple institutions and industry partners to ensure that the brightest and most knowledgeable minds are engaged by the critical problems and to achieve the best solutions. We may also find useful guidance for structuring a center in our campus' experience of managing Brookhaven National Laboratory, which is one of the DOE's premier non-weapons research facilities, with an annual budget close to $400 million. The trustees of Brookhaven Science Associates, the corporate management entity, include representatives of the major user institutions as well as Stony Brook and Battelle Memorial Institute, the two management partners.

Based on my work over the last eight months as chair of the SUNY Chancellor's Infrastructure Task Force (CITF), I would also recommend that the center organization should allow for a degree of flexibility. In SUNY, we have formed a loose but coherent network of SUNY campuses—and there are many—with relevant research and instructional capacities. It would be straightforward, for example, to incorporate the remaining public and private colleges and universities into this network. We and the other academic institutions already partner with the federal laboratories in the state. The model that we have adopted in the CITF is that new knowledge that is obtained through research programs will be incorporated into the educational curricula for graduate and undergraduate students and into workforce training programs that are currently offered by two and four year colleges to retrain workers with outdated skills and for continuing education and professional development. Stony Brook has successfully deployed numerous workforce training programs in conjunction with the municipal and State departments of labor and of economic development, and we are about to open the campus' first off-site training facility—targeting the software industry—in Long Island's first "smart building," the former Grumman electronics division facility that has been reborn as the Long Island Business and Technology Center in Great River. Our dean's council as well as disciplinary advisory committees of industry representatives has given us broad experience in incorporating industry response and input into the continuing design and reshaping of our teaching curriculum.

We have a proven track record in technology transfer and the model employed in the SUNY system—where New York companies receive first crack at licensing new technologies and the advantage of licensing to a start-up versus an established company is always carefully examined—is worth considering for the national cyber centers. In FY2000, the most recent year for which comparative data are available, the Association of University Technology Managers ranked SUNY in the top 15 nationally, ahead of such venerable research powerhouses as Harvard and Johns Hopkins. Because I have to toot Stony Brook's horn at times like this, I am proud to report that Stony Brook generated 95 percent of the more than $16 million in licensing revenues that propelled SUNY to this ranking. Our campus is the source of the only two drugs that have yet been licensed for sale in the U.S. by the FDA, and our Office of Technology Licensing has accounted for between 30 percent and 70 percent of all SUNY invention disclosures, licenses, patent applications, and issued patents in each of the last five years. Some 21 new companies have been started based on Stony Brook technologies and a significant portion of them are occupants of the Long Island High Technology Incubator on our campus; we expect to see more in our software incubator and in the new incubator we will be managing, to be constructed at the former Grumman test flight facility in Calverton. New enterprise creation is a key tool of technology-based economic development and any cyber research center should demonstrate a strong connection to an incubation program.

In closing, I would like to congratulate the Committee on its vision and its leadership in driving forward this critical cyber security initiative. You have determined an absolutely fundamental need for our national defense and have created a superb opportunity for New York's and our nation's leading edge academic and industrial researchers to act immediately to conduct the necessary research for new cyber security strategies and technologies to move quickly into implementation, with continuous training—where our nation and our State, especially the industries that are such an important part of our State economy, need them so urgently.

Biography for Yacov Shamash

Dr. Shamash is Vice President for Economic Development and the Dean of the College of Engineering and Applied Sciences and the Harriman School for Management and Policy at SUNY Stony Brook. The College has over 2,000 undergraduate and 750 graduate students. In 1994 he initiated the highly successful state-wide SPIR program (Strategic Partnership for Industrial Resurgence). During the past eight years, working through the SPIR program, the College has partnered with more than 220 companies to assist them with more than 1150 projects, and to help them attract over 83 million dollars of federal grants. Under his leadership, external research funding in the College has almost tripled.

Prior to joining SUNY Stony Brook in 1992, Dr. Shamash served as the Director of the School of Electrical Engineering and Computer Science at Washington State University and was responsible for the establishment of a National Science Foundation Industry/University Center for the Design of Analog/Digital Integrated Circuits. He developed a consortium of three universities, fifteen high technology companies (including Boeing, HP, Tektronics, Mentor Graphics and others), the State of Washington and NSF, to create the Center.

Dr. Shamash has a great deal of experience in dealing with high technology companies. He has been a member of the Board of Directors of KeyTronic since 1989 and American Medical Alert since 2001. He is also on the Boards of Directors of a number of start-up companies and serves on the Boards of not-for-profit organizations such as the Long Island High Technology Incubator (LIHTI), the Long Island Forum for Technology (LIFT) and the Long Island Software Technology Network (LISTnet). He is a Fellow of the IEEE.

He has held faculty positions at Florida Atlantic University, the University of Pennsylvania and Tel Aviv University. He received his undergraduate and graduate degrees from Imperial College of Science and Technology in London, England.

Dr. Shamash has authored over 110 technical publications and received research funding from numerous sources, including industry, State and Federal agencies.

STONY BROOK
STATE UNIVERSITY OF NEW YORK

Office of the Dean
College of Engineering and Applied Sciences

January 13, 2003

Chairman Sherwood Boehlert
US House of Representatives
Committee on Science
Suite 2320 Rayburn House Office Building
Washington, DC 20515-6301

Dear Congressman Boehlert:

Please be advised that I have not received nor do I currently receive federal funding pertaining to the subject matter on which I testified before the committee in Rome, New York on June 12, 2002.

Sincerely yours,

Yacov Shamash
Dean

YS:jk

STONY BROOK, NEW YORK 11794-2200 TEL: 631-632-8380 FAX: 631-632-8205

Chairman BOEHLERT. And our final witness for today, Mr. Michael Miravalle, President and CEO of Dolphin Technologies, Incorporated, which is an exciting economic success story in Central New York in the high technology field.

Welcome.

STATEMENT OF MR. MICHAEL A. MIRAVALLE, PRESIDENT AND CEO, DOLPHIN TECHNOLOGIES, INC., ROME, NEW YORK

Mr. MIRAVALLE. Mr. Chairman, Members of the Committee. Thank you. I'm honored to be here today. I will very briefly summarize my testimony. I would ask that it be entered in its entirety into the record, and I would like to bring a bit of business perspective to the testimony today.

If I had a theme to my testimony and the points I'd like to make this morning, it's let's unleash our brain power. Let's remove the constraints that hold them in check. I look to you. I plead with you to let us put our best and brightest together to work regardless of where they are in the public or private sector or academia.

I have been in business 36 years. I have not over those years—I have never seen it fail when you put the right people together, give them a common objective regardless of where they are or who they work for, and say, "Go get them," they do it. Amazing things happen. And so that's the gist of this testimony this morning.

I also agree that New York State is uniquely positioned because of its academic, its industry institutions as well as its government organizations and it also has the financial capital of the free world.

As with any research agenda, I believe it's important to have a model. You can not solve the entire problem for the world or the country in one bite. So let's take one piece of that apple. Let's make it the Big Apple, and let's try to build a model and come up with a research agenda in this state that can work nationwide in how we would partner our public and private organizations and academic organizations.

I think it's critically important that we form a team from those different sectors to come up with a research agenda. That research agenda should have two parts to it. What is the research that's needed to fulfill our short-term and long-term goals and objectives in cyber security? But also it needs to have a tech transition. As my colleague Yakov points out, all the research in the world is of minimal value if it never gets out of the research community. That doesn't happen without a technology transition process, and that also takes money to fund that.

I also believe that we need to look at what we have—and I was very encouraged by Dr. Engle's comments about being able to look within the technology community of different Federal sectors such as the Department of Defense, in particular the United States Air Force, which I was very proud to serve for a number of years on active duty. We have a tremendous amount of technology in our military services that is directly applicable to law enforcement.

One of the things that my company does is it has a foot in multiple doors. We have clients in the Department of Defense, the intelligence community and the Department of Justice and law enforcement. It's disconcerting, to say the least, to see the needs of one community or another when you find a piece of technology that is ideally suited to meeting the needs of another community but because of what we've talked about and what has been testified here in committee, it's almost impossible, if not impossible, to get that piece of technology to the organization that needs it because it was developed by somebody else even though it was a dead fit.

Let's fix that. Let's let our best and brightest work together. Let's start smooth flowing things that fit. And again, within the context of protecting national security under classified processes, if we have capabilities in the United States Air Force that can help the New York State police, if we have capabilities in the Marine Corps that can help the Secret Service, let's start looking at how we get that technology and share it. We've already bought and paid for it once. It's the property of the American taxpayer. Let's not reinvent the wheel from a technology standpoint.

That would lead me into one of my final points, that's the ingenuity of the American people. We have examples of that in our homes. We've seen that. It's gone on for years. We develop something, say, for military application. Within a few years of turning that technology, that military capability over to our entrepreneurial community of the United States, they make new products we never even thought of. Titanium alloys are now in fishing lures. Certainly the research wasn't intended for that. But that's the kind of entrepreneurial spirit coupled with ingenuity that I think we need in cyber security.

Let's take products that we have that we built for one thing, let's turn them back to private industry. If we've developed and made an investment in country in certain technology that we've now decided maybe don't fit with why we did that research, we're not going to apply it or perhaps it's an outdated version of that research, turn it back to the companies that built it. If the United States government isn't going to use it, give it back to the people that did it. My suspicion is they will find a whole new application that we never thought of to use that technology for. That's the type of spark that we're going to need in the cyber security war that we're in.

I would also quickly like to mention Dr. Engle's comments about the war fighters. And, again, looking at the technology transition potential, I would submit those of us that are in the cyber security war are all war fighters and that these tools are not linked just to active duty military that are deployed on foreign soil defending our nation's interest but they equally apply to Mr. Weaver's special agents, that patrolman that stopped a terrorist on a highway. We're all in it together. This is our war. We're all in the same situation.

So let's dust off our shelves. Let's find the things that we have that can help. Let's give them back to the people that are equipped to do something with it.

From an industry perspective, one of the ironies—I think the comment was made there were only eight Ph.D.s awarded in this country in information assurance recently. One of the challenges that we face collectively from an industry perspective is we want to send people to Cordon Bleu Culinary Cooking School, but when they return to their homes, we offer them jobs in fast food burger joints.

We need to take a hard look at what we're doing with our computer science majors, in particular when they specialize in information assurance. It's a very narrow field. It's a very highly compensated field for a select few number of individuals and the compensation is tied largely to the geographic areas in which they work, and so what we see is a brain drain from our communities to a few large metropolitan areas.

If we find that, again, this war is going to be fought on the home front as we talked about, we need to be able to reach out and create the job opportunities for these students when they do graduate to increase the number of students that want to major in these specific fields.

In my opinion, if we, the industry, don't create the job opportunities, then the students aren't going to take the curriculum that's required to get into that job opportunity. We the industry can't create the job opportunity unless somebody creates the work like H.R. 3394 has done.

That generates work. Work generates jobs. Jobs create opportunities. The students go on to those opportunities, and that's the cycle that we have to implement here.

In closing, I think we face a challenge unlike any that we've ever encountered in our history. We have proliferated information technology in every dimension of our life. What we've also created is a tremendous Achilles heel.

We haven't even scratched the surface on research in information assurance. In fact, we're only looking at half the problem. We're only addressing how to protect our systems. For the most part, we don't have a clue what's inside the systems we're protecting or how it even got there.

So this is a field that will not change. It will not stagnate. And we are combating an adversary that is just as agile and just as dedicated to staying one step ahead of us.

So let's unleash the brilliance of our people. Let's cut them loose. Let's put them to work. Let's give them the opportunity to show us what they can do.

Thank you, Mr. Chairman.

[The prepared statement of Mr. Miravalle follows:]

PREPARED STATEMENT OF MICHAEL A. MIRAVALLE

I think that it is vitally important that we recognize New York State faces the same challenges, albeit on a smaller scale, that our national-level endeavors must address. Foremost among those challenges is the institutionalized bureaucratic process that severely constraints, or prohibits entirely, organizations from different public sectors freely cooperating and working together to achieve common objectives. Alignment by academic institutions and private sector companies with specific Federal and State organizations further fragments our technology community and compounds the challenges we face. Recognizing that there are valid reasons, ranging from funding sources to public law, for this "enclaving effect," I think we should set these constraints aside and explore what could be done versus why it cannot be done. New York State is an excellent model with virtually every type of public, private, and academic institution represented. Let's use New York as our innovation baseline. Let's remove the less important "rules and regulations" from the exploratory undertakings of our good thinkers and empower them with a clean slate. Let's challenge them to create a New York State model of what could and should be done independent of entrenched mind-sets, risk-adverse management structures, and bureaucratic "turf" disputes. Let's use that model to identify those things that need to be changed, and that we have the power to change, that inhibit us from fully engaging the extraordinary talent, skill, and dedication of our most powerful asset—

our own people. How can New York industry, academia, Federal laboratories, and State organizations work more effectively with law enforcement? Let's begin with minimizing, or eliminating completely, the institutional roadblocks that prevent a free and open exchange of ideas and sharing of capabilities. Let's reward innovative thinking and creativity. Let's get the right people from the right organizations together and support them.

I think an important first step is to view the Air Force Research Laboratory's Information Directorate and National Institute of Justice's Cyber Science Laboratory, both located in Rome, as a tightly coupled resource. Both the academic institutions and companies that support each Laboratory should also be viewed as part of that resource. In effect, we create a single, virtual entity that is chartered to focus on developing our New York State model. Thanks to Congressman's Boehlert's bill on Cyber Security Research and Development (H.R. 3394), I believe we now have a unique enabler that will allow development of a multi-agency agenda for that model encompassing basic research through fielding and maintenance of homeland defense, law enforcement and information sharing capabilities. The agenda should address existing technologies that can be of immediate value, near-term efforts that will produce needed capabilities in the next one to two years, and technology gaps requiring R&D. Development of the agenda should be accomplished by a team composed of representatives from both laboratories and the law enforcement community. Underwriting this agenda should be a well-resourced technology transfer process that puts capabilities into the hands of practitioners and provides life-cycle support to include installation and training. The agenda and technology transfer plan should be reviewed, validated, and implemented by the appropriate authority for each of the participants. Both the agenda and technology transfer plan should be designed to "smooth flow" capabilities to end-user communities regardless of originating organization. I believe we can use H.R. 3394 as the catalyst to partner diverse organizations across the public and private sector and reward them for forming such alliances. Let's broaden the term "dual-use technology" from just government/commercial to now include military/law enforcement or intelligence/public security. Let's encourage and reward such R&D undertakings through the budgetary process. I sincerely believe that the most effective way to bring New York industry, academia, government, and law enforcement organizations together is to create a sanctioned, resourced environment that encourages and rewards our "best and brightest" from each sector to work together as a team with a single common objective. If it works in New York State, perhaps it can work across the Nation.

Another important aspect of innovative research and development is the "ingenuity" factor resident in the private sector. Our nation has a long history of developing advanced products and capabilities for military and/or government applications. When these breakthroughs are released into the public domain, entrepreneurial ingenuity takes over and new commercial applications are developed. Titanium alloys for military aircraft are now used on fishing lures. Plexiglas, Teflon, silicon lubricants are all commonplace in our homes. Within the constraints of national security, I believe we should reach into our reservoir of government-owned information technologies and provide private industry an opportunity to innovate and market. The Air Force Research Laboratory Information Directorate has a wealth of technologies that, for a variety of reasons, are not going to make their way into the operational community. In many cases, R&D prototypes were used to explore specific concepts that were later abandoned by the military or the prototype revealed conceptual flaws. Most of this work was accomplished by private industry via government contracts. If the government is not going to use this technology, then let's return it to the developer and relinquish all rights. While there are certainly formal programs in place, such as Small Business Innovative Research efforts and Dual Use Science and Technology programs, that provide an opportunity for private industry to develop commercial products in conjunction with government needs and with government funding assistance, I would suggest that we add a straightforward process that simply returns technologies to developers that the government is not going to use. This process could also apply to obsolete versions of capabilities no longer supported or used by the military. Obviously, such a process must function within the constraints of national security and U.S. Laws. We certainly don't want to put our most sensitive technologies currently in use, or planned for use, on the "open" market. On the other hand, let's "dust off our shelves" and give private industry an opportunity to explore new markets and alternative applications for capabilities that are no longer destined for operational deployment.

I would like to point out that the co-location of the NIJ Cyber Science Laboratory with the Air Force Research Laboratory Information Directorate creates a unique opportunity to showcase DOD and Air Force-developed technologies to a previously inaccessible law enforcement community and their academic and private sector partners. I believe this greatly expands the opportunity to transfer government-owned technology to private sector organizations. We have an excellent opportunity to leverage our nation's investment in military information technology research by augmenting the law enforcement and public security technology base with the results of such research. I also believe implementing such a cross-fertilization program between the two Laboratories will serve as a magnet for private industry supporting both communities. Companies with a law enforcement customer base can come to Rome and benefit from the technology transfer process. Companies representing the current industry base supporting military R&D at Rome can expand their market into the law enforcement community.

There are many fine Information Assurance and Cyber Security institutes and consortiums being formed around the Nation. However, I believe the nationally-unique juxtaposition of the Air Force Research Laboratory Information Directorate, the NIJ Cyber Science Laboratory, the private industry base, and the many excellent academic institutions in Central New York represents one of the strongest foundations in the country for birthing a "CyberScience Valley." This foundation is our "engine." H.R. 3394 is our "fuel." Our collective challenge is to harness the "horsepower" for both the good of the nation and our community. Cyber security is an extraordinarily diverse and well-compensated profession. It is a continually evolving field that generates numerous spin-off professions and technology paths for new products and services. It is a field that must continually respond to new and greater threats from an equally dedicated adversary community. Unless the civilized world decides to abandon the use of computers, it is a field that will never become obsolete or stagnate. Cyber security permeates the fabric of our society, even in our homes. Our challenge is to use our unique Central New York foundation to generate the work that creates the jobs that attracts the professionals who, in turn, attract more professionals. This process applies to public sector organizations, academic institutions, and private industry. One proactive step we can collectively take to enhance our opportunity for economic growth in cyber security is to recognize that cyber security professionals are well-educated, well-compensated individuals that are highly marketable. . .and usually mobile to extent they will seek the optimum employment package versus the optimum geographic location. We need to shed our image of a low-paying place to live. We need to recognize that we are not going to be competitive in attracting top professionals when the best we can offer them is a compensation package amounting to half, or less, of what they can make somewhere else. If we want to attract and grow a thriving professional community in the information security field, then we must recognize that our local organizations—public, private, academic—must have the financial ability to attract and retain this community.

In addition to attracting top professionals to live and work in our Central New York cyber security community, we must also grow and retain our own talent. I think this is less a problem of our schools and universities providing the appropriate curriculum for a skilled work force and more a problem of the perceived lack of opportunities to include the previously mentioned compensation problem. I do think we have an excellent opportunity to expand the partnering of local private industry with our colleges and universities to form teams to pursue cyber security work. This has the synergistic effect of exposing students and faculty to hard-core, real-world challenges that must be met and overcome while exposing industry professionals to fresh ways of approaching problems and developing solutions. I also think that providing opportunities for our local young people to work side-by-side with professionals on real world applications occasionally changes their minds about remaining in the area following graduation, particularly if they have a good job opportunity that affords them the ability to continue exploring and working in the areas that they found interesting. I firmly believe that by creating local employment opportunities with appropriate compensation levels and establishing the prestige of working in a nationally-recognized cyber science community, we can retain many of our young people.

In conclusion, I would like to thank you for affording me this opportunity to express my views. Our nation faces a challenge unlike any we have encountered in our history. Our development, proliferation, and reliance on information technology have enabled us to accomplish great things and enjoy a wonderful way of life. Unfortunately, it has also created an Achilles heel that we are just beginning to understand. I have great faith in the dedication, inventiveness, and brilliance of our people. Let's work together to give them the opportunity to show what they can do.

BIOGRAPHY FOR MICHAEL A. MIRAVALLE

Michael A. Miravalle, the President, CEO, and founder of Dolphin Technology, has over thirty-six years of experience in the Intelligence and Security fields. He has served in the United States Air Force, providing operational, tactical intelligence during combat operations and worked closely with the military of several nations developing tactical intelligence operations. As a U.S. Government civilian, Mr. Miravalle was the Director of the Command and Control, Communications, and Intelligence Systems Development and Integration Office for Pacific Air Forces. He has developed and implemented numerous multinational intelligence information architectures focused on supporting direct combat operations. He has authored international security policies for the Office of Secretary of Defense, the Joint Chiefs of Staff, and the Air Force. He directly supports the Defense Advanced Research Projects Agency for developing international technology research agendas and evaluating resultant capabilities for transition to operational organizations. He also serves as Chairman of the Board for the Griffiss Institute for Information Assurance.

DolphinTechnology INCORPORATED

Chairman Sherwood Boehlert
US House of Representatives
Committee on Science
Suite 2320 Rayburn House Office Building
Washington, DC 20515-6301

February 13, 2003

Dear Mr. Boehlert,

Please be advised that I have received the following federal funding pertaining to the subject matter on which I testified before the committee in Utica, NY on July 2002.

National Institute of Justice funding during the period Dec 01- Mar 03

$1,976,864.20 for Law Enforcement Intelligence support, Cyber Science analysis,NIJ Center requirements analysis and technical assistance, and AGILE test and Evaluation

Department of Defense funding during the period Feb 01 – Jun 03

$4,110,904.00 for ISSE Guard development, installation, maintenance, documentation, training, and research. ISSE Guard is a boundary control technology that enables the direct digital coupling of intelligence networks with other networks of lower classification levels or networks of other nations.

Sincerely,

Michael A. Miravalle
President and CEO

474 Phoenix Drive – Rome, New York 13441-4911 – 315 838-7000 – 315 838-7096 fax – www.dolphtech.com

PANEL II: DISCUSSION

Chairman BOEHLERT. Thank you, and I've got a question of you right off the bat.

Mr. MIRAVALLE. Yes, sir.

Chairman BOEHLERT. Keep that mike.

GROWTH POTENTIAL FOR THE INFORMATION SECURITY FIELD IN CENTRAL NEW YORK

Take a look into your crystal ball and give us some projections. What do you see as a potential for growth right here in the Central New York area in the field of information security?

Mr. MIRAVALLE. I think the growth potential is tremendous because of the coupling of the Air Force Research Lab with the National Institute of Justice Cyberscience Lab with the academic institutions that we have.

We can create, for lack of a better term, a Cybersecurity Valley similar to a Silicon Valley. Today, there is no geographic area in the world for that matter, let alone in the country, that specializes in just this domain nor do they have the resident assets that are just waiting to be coupled together, bringing together Department of Justice, Department of Defense laboratories in the same physical space as what you have in Rome coupled with the universities in programs like Utica College that have e-crime programs that are all within a small geographic area.

I think there's tremendous growth potential in this area. It's very fragmented. Information assurance today in the economic community is fragmented and splintered. There is no one place where it comes together.

Chairman BOEHLERT. I want to personally thank you on behalf of the community at large for your role——

Mr. MIRAVALLE. Thank you.

Chairman BOEHLERT.—in trying to bring all this together, working with our office and Utica College and a number of others in the community at large that share a common vision, and you ain't seen nothing yet.

Mr. MIRAVALLE. I agree with you.

TRANSFER OF SECRET SERVICE INTO DHS

Chairman BOEHLERT. Mr. Weaver, how do you think the shift is going to be for your office into the new Department of Homeland Security? Do you have some speculation on that?

And let me ask you further, because you are so very familiar with what we're doing up in Rome with the NIJ Cyber-Science Lab. What kind of a role do you see for that laboratory?

Mr. WEAVER. Well, the concept that we have in the task force, which I directly attribute to my director, Brian Stafford, is taking a public position in support of the President that this is an exciting opportunity to move to homeland security. He would like to go intact as an agent and not break apart and bring all of our tools and resources over to help our mission, the country's mission, national security, information security, national security special events and all the special projects and resources that the service has. We are a very streamlined agency. We have some very good powerful tools to bring to bear for the country. We see homeland security as an exciting opportunity.

ROLE OF THE NIJ CYBER-SCIENCE LAB AT ROME IN THE NEW DHS

Chairman BOEHLERT. What about the NIJ Cyber-Science Lab at Rome? You are familiar with that. Do you see a role for that facility in this new department?

Mr. WEAVER. As I've seen some of the preliminary drafts—and I'm not the expert on it, but I've just received information on it. I have seen some breakout groups specifically designed for state and local. I think that's a very important component. If you look at crime and cyber crime, 80 percent of it some might say is on the state and local level, and it's got to play a significant role in this environment.

I saw some charts—and I was pleased to see that. I don't know if it will hold up as it moves forward, but it was an exciting organizational chart with state and local and NIJ. Its charter is right there.

Chairman BOEHLERT. Thank you very much.

Ms. Jackson Lee.

Ms. JACKSON LEE. Thank you very much, Mr. Chairman.

Cyber security is going on right now, (referring to cell phone ringing) but in any event, it stops shortly. It stops on its own accord.

Let me thank the witnesses for their very instructive testimony, and you touch on a number of areas that we should take back to Washington, and I would like to probe some of those based upon your testimony.

First of all, Mr. Weaver, let me thank you generally for the service of the Secret Service. And as the Chairman has so eloquently expressed tribute to the flag that sits behind us, might I add a tribute, too. It looks as if it's a flag that survived, that has the insignia of the U.S. Secret Service, so that is a double symbol, if you will, that, one, we can do this and we can survive. So I appreciate it very much.

Obviously, the Secret Service is one of the newer law enforcement agencies, I might think, in terms of its history, and I think it's important to note the very special role that the Secret Service played in our survival on September 11, not only your services but certainly those who were assigned to the president of the United States. And it certainly is important to keep the commander in chief with the ability to provide leadership and guidance, and they were very pivotal in that role as he was away from Washington, D.C., and I think it's very important to note.

IMPORTANCE OF INFORMATION SHARING

You have spoken about, I believe, a task force that you have formulated here in the New York area that you are a part of, and I think that is key. I could not miss the opportunity to ask you to comment on information sharing. Certainly you know that many of our committees in Washington right now are looking at the issues of information sharing as related to September 11, and I can't help but think that cyber security issues are interwoven.

But I would like your comment on information sharing, the importance of it. And you commented on your excitement about the Homeland Security Department as it makes its way through Congress. But what does it say to you or how do you respond to the FBI and the CIA not at this time being part of the homeland security? I raise that to you.

And let me quickly ask questions that Dr. Shamash and the representative from the private sector would be kind enough to answer. When you talk about the national security cyber security center, what role does it play in collaborating with the private sector? What role would it play?

And then I would appreciate very much Mr. Miravalle expanding on a very creative idea of giving back—dormant, I imagine is what he is saying—technology that the government has and how that excites and motivates and helps create in the private sector?

And, again, thank you for your service.

Mr. WEAVER. Congresswoman Jackson Lee, I sincerely appreciate your pointing out that there was a banner that made it out—it was actually blown out of the building. That's why it survived the intensity of that day and was recovered—the Secret Service banner behind me. It serves as an inspiration to the young men and women in public service and so it means a lot to us.

Information sharing. Before all this happened, we were doing this in New York because the industry came to us, and we created a bond with them for the sharing of information, not designed on the criminal response but designed on what was the right thing to do for the community, what was in the best interest of the business. We found that due diligence and best practices was underscored with this systemic approach, and all the preventive and proactive things that we do gave us a good skill set for information sharing.

We're small, but that's our strength. We have to partner with state and local and with the private sector and with the military. We cannot do it all by ourself, and so it puts us into an environment to develop very, very significant skill sets on the protection side of our house and on the investigative side of our house that rewards information sharing within our culture.

This is ingrained in you and incubated in you throughout your career so when you come under stress in tough times that you do it instinctively; you don't have to be told to do it, and it works, and you work well with it. And then you take that, and it's high maintenance, but it has a force multiplier to it. There's nothing better than to see talented people together as Mike Miravalle pointed out, doing what's self-satisfying in achieving significant goals.

So the information sharing is (inaudible) lip-served. Typically what people will do within the financial community in New York City is they will connect through the task force which is just a facilitator, an enabler, and then they will go off-line and they will do a side bar to take care of business. I think it's great that we can facilitate that environment.

As far as the second part of your question to me, whether the FBI and CIA are not in homeland security, and why is that? I don't recall being invited to the policy decision-making process.

[Laughter.]

But from afar, I will tell you that repositioning agencies is just one part of the equation from my perspective. Reforming and drawing down and making them all seamless and removing the stovepipes and independent action is. If we have another day like Pearl Harbor and like September 11, those kind of things will not serve us well.

And so we must change how we do business and you have a great responsibility and my full support and our agency's full support about how best to do that. So I would put that back to your attention that there is much work to do. And I think that this committee, this strong committee, can make a big difference in how that information sharing does develop. Okay.

Chairman BOEHLERT. Thank you.

Ms. JACKSON LEE. Thank you.

Dr. Shamash.

INDUSTRY COLLABORATION WITH A CYBER SECURITY CENTER

Dr. SHAMASH. Thank you. In terms of industry working with a cyber security center, I think it's critical that—and we found this from a number of other initiatives that we've taken. Leveraging of resources is absolutely critical, not only leveraging of financial resources but also intellectual resources.

There are a lot of businesses and software companies that are doing some dynamite work in this area. There are a lot of academicians that are doing some fantastic work in this area. There is some terrific work going on in Rome labs in this area.

If we're going to try and capitalize and put our best foot forward, it's critical that we bring everybody in to work together,and we have models that have demonstrated that that can work. So you get leverage of intellectual capability and you get leverage of financial resources, also. And you do that by having an advisory board, an industrial advisory board, that can help govern the research and development work that goes on in the center.

If you don't have industry participation, you can have some of the best research work done, and it will never see the light of day, and so I think it's absolutely important to get the business community involved right at the start and not only setting the agenda but also benefiting from the tech transfer that will occur afterwards.

Ms. JACKSON LEE. Thank you.

Mr. MIRAVALLE. I think—and I will bring the business side to this in terms of—let's put it on the table, "profit"—for profit. Businesses are in business to make money. That leads me to a couple of points. One is———

Ms. JACKSON LEE. We want you to make money, please.

Mr. MIRAVALLE. Because then I can hire his staff who can go to work for the Secret Service.

Ms. JACKSON LEE. Absolutely.

Mr. MIRAVALLE. I think it's important to incentivize folks, and I think different parts of the community are incentivized by different things. And so I would like to just make two quick points.

One is I think that good people enjoy working together regardless of whether they are in industry or academia. We're a very proud member of the Electronic Crimes Task Force. We see that in all of his meetings where people kind of shed the cloak of who they are working for and they get together and kind of agree to help each other in spite of the organizations they work for. We ought to formalize that process, for one, so you see that with industry, as well. Now it's not sponsored by the Secret Service. It's independent and they go off on their own.

But also I think that you can incentivize and reward—and award work based on partnering. So that today, in today's climate, for example, when private industry competes for work from the Federal Government, they classically go through some type of an RFP process and submit a proposal, and there are generally teammates. Generally, those teammates are other industry partners. It's not out of the realm of possibility to say, "Look, one of the criteria for awarding it has to be an industry and a school." And you would get more points when you compete for work if your team is so and so technology and so and so university, as opposed to two so and so technologies. Those are the kinds of things that I believe you can start doing to encourage them to partner.

The bottom line is the job opportunities, ultimately the goal, are in industry and that's what really needs to be grown. That's where the work is. If we're going to grow this, that's where it has to occur.

Chairman BOEHLERT. Thank you very much.

Ms. JACKSON LEE. Thank you.

Chairman BOEHLERT. Mr. Smith.

Mr. MIRAVALLE. I'm sorry, I believe you had a second question.

Chairman BOEHLERT. I didn't mean to be precipitous here.

GOVERNMENT RELINQUISHMENT OF DORMANT RESEARCH

Ms. JACKSON LEE. Quickly, and I thank you. It was your creative idea about what lays dormant in the Federal Government and how we draw it out so that industry can utilize it.

Mr. MIRAVALLE. Very briefly, if we're not going to use it, why not give it back to the people that built it? They built it under a Federal contract or a state contract, it's not going anywhere but has potential. Just relinquish all government rights. Whatever they want to do with it,let them do it.

Ms. JACKSON LEE. Appreciate the thought. Thank you very much.

Chairman BOEHLERT. Could you think about it—you probably can't do it right off the top of your head—a specific example or two?

Mr. MIRAVALLE. In the R&D field, in particular, you will build prototypes to validate research, and sometimes they will validate a particular concept. For example—I will give you a specific example. There was a point where they thought about equipping—Department of Defense, specifically the Secretary of Defense, thought about equipping small units such as Rangers, Marines and Special Forces Operations with a small PDA-based land for combat scenarios to exchange information. They kind of moved away from that concept, but several companies were involved in developing that technology.

They moved away from it because it wasn't suitable for military combat scenarios. Perhaps that technology could be used for law enforcement organizations. It's basically a laptop based command center. I was privileged to see a demo. My company was not involved with that project whatsoever. But it's not going anywhere. It's just going to sit. So give it back to the companies that built it. Maybe the police can use it or the Secret Service.

Chairman BOEHLERT. Thank you. Thank you very much.

Mr. Smith.

Mr. SMITH. Mr. Chairman, thank you.

Gentlemen, thank you for giving your time today.

I want to talk a little bit about the best, the most capable, the brightest.

RECRUITING/RETAINING ENGINEERING PROFESSIONALS

Mr. Shamash. Dean, how many of your engineering students that seek graduate work for their master's or doctorate are foreign students? Give me an estimate.

Dr. SHAMASH. At the graduate level———

Mr. SMITH. At the graduate level.

Dr. SHAMASH. At the graduate level, it's about 50, 55 percent.

Mr. SMITH. I think that's an indication, number 1, that our university system, certainly Stony Brook, is the best in the world, and a lot of other countries send their best and the brightest here to this country to perfect their education in the sciences and the math and the engineering.

Do you—the INS has tightened up after graduation. So, in the past, where we have utilized the talent of foreign students to help in our industry and our economy and in the past they have all selected to stay in this country and be part of our production, productivity, development, now INS is tightening up and saying, "Look, the minute you graduate, get out of here. You got to go back to your own country." Is that a—do you see that as a problem?

Dr. SHAMASH. I think that could be a problem. Again, I think the data that I had was something like 80 percent of the students that graduated at foreign university—foreign students graduating from our universities, about 80 percent of them stayed here, which is a tremendous intellectual resource, and I would hate to lose that.

Mr. SMITH. You're losing it right now, I understand. INS has really tightened up.

Dr. SHAMASH. We may lose—I'm hoping that if a student graduates, has a job in industry, you know, whether we can do some of the background security checks on that individual, that that individual would still be hired. I'm hopeful.

Mr. SMITH. I want to make that point because it is a problem that I've talked to in other schools that they are losing some of these bright foreign students.

The other flip side of that is the danger of some of the most—well, two flip sides. One is we're failing in our science and math tests in our worldwide test. We're not doing a good job compared to the rest of the industrialized world or the rest of much of the nonindustrialized world. We've got to do a better job.

In our Subcommittee on Research, we've had several hearings. And so what do we do to get more of our American students interested involved?

One of my questions to one of my panels was, to the extent that education in the kindergarten through 12 grade is more the lighting of a fire, inspiring, rather than the filling of a container with information, where is this fire lit for science and math?

And the overwhelming response was probably between three years old and eight years old because if they are not interested or they get turned off by their parents or by a teacher, then it's unlikely they are going to pursue it. Of course, you need to kindle that fire with quality teachers through high school.

Let me ask you another estimate question.

What percentage of the numbers that enter engineering in their freshman year of college at your school will dropout or change majors?

Dr. SHAMASH. Change majors from engineering?

Mr. SMITH. Dropout or change majors from engineering.

Dr. SHAMASH. I would say probably about 50 percent.

Mr. SMITH. 50 percent. Is that a failure———

Dr. SHAMASH. From the freshman level. No, I don't think it's a failure because a lot of the students have come in thinking that they want to be engineers really don't want to be engineers.

Mr. SMITH. Is that a problem? I don't mean to concentrate on what you're doing as Dean and how you're failing by not reapproving this. Because this is similar to what I hear from other schools.

We just had a hearing with University of Michigan, Michigan State. We've got to do a better job of making that interesting, making that challenging, and how do we do that?

Dr. SHAMASH. I think some of the things that we already are doing through the National Science Foundation, the number of programs for improving undergraduate teaching in the sciences and engineering, certainly have been extremely helpful. I think we're going to see some more of that.

I believe this committee, Mr. Chairman———

Chairman BOEHLERT. Yes, we have a bill. Quite frankly, Dr. Shamash, I thought that my distinguished colleague was just sort of setting you up so you could then brag on the good work the Committee is doing. Because under Chairman Smith's leadership on the Subcommittee, we have put the NSF on a path to double its budget in a 5-year period, and Congress is standing up and applauding, and it's passed by a significant margin, and we are the authors of this committee on the Science and Math Partnership.

I'm now taking your time. I'll give you more time.

But the Science and Math Partnership, which is a vital portion of the President's *No Child Left Behind* legislation, because this committee recognizes, thanks to the testimony from experts like you, and Mr. Miravalle from the private sector, telling us what they need and the shortfall we have. We did author that portion of the President's *No Child Left Behind Program* called the Science and Math Partnership.

So, Mr. Smith, you sort of set the stage for this.

Mr. SMITH. Hopefully, we're looking at how to perfect that, because it's good legislation.

Mr. Miravalle, in terms of putting the smartest and the brightest together—Bin Laden, for example, is not a dummy, as we well know, now. He's extremely capable. He's brought in the best psychologists and the best mathematicians and engineers.

If a company called Protect Against Cyber Security—I mean Bin Laden wants to bring the brightest and the smartest together to fill out his quest to damage us. What about hiring the best and the brightest? If a company called some good name, Better Protection for America, came to an individual graduating with a doctorate degree and said, "Look, we want to develop the best guard against cyber security, but first we want to see just how good a system anybody could develop to hack into national security or our military and we're going to up the salary of anybody else. We'll give you $150,000 a year to start for developing the kinds of things that we need to guard against."

I'm not saying, but maybe this is a terrorist group. Our students would take that job, probably, wouldn't they?

Mr. MIRAVALLE. Yes. I think we do that to some extent in our research community today with organizations like DARPA and Rome Laboratory, where we do research initiatives like private industry to try to build a bulletproof system. There's a whole process called red teaming, where we take people—and the kids love these kinds of jobs—to attack other systems and try to find vulnerabilities.

Mr. SMITH. No, I'm saying Bin Laden is hiring these people.

Mr. MIRAVALLE. Oh, you're saying he's hiring them?

Mr. SMITH. Yes. One hundred fifty thousand, right out of school. "We want you to work for us and give us your talent."

Mr. MIRAVALLE. Well, I'm not sure how you legislate patriotism.

Mr. SMITH. But no, no, my question was the probability of that student taking that job for $150,000? I mean he doesn't know it's Bin Laden. All he knows is it's a company that has———

Mr. MIRAVALLE. A very real possibility. Absolutely. Absolutely. We don't know that that's not going on already.

Mr. SMITH. That's right.

Mr. MIRAVALLE. We don't know that that's not happening. That's part of the problem we have in cyber security. I mean we import anything into our systems. We protect them from attack from outside, but what we put in them—we download from the web, from web sites from different countries around the globe. We have no idea what's in that software.

Mr. SMITH. It's a challenge.

Mr. Chairman, thank you.

Chairman BOEHLERT. Thank you very much.

Dr. Bartlett.

Mr. BARTLETT. Thank you very much.

PROTECTING THE NATION'S INFRASTRUCTURE AGAINST A NUCLEAR EMP

I want to return for a moment to the theme of my questions to the first panel. When I mention nuclear EMP, a lot of people never heard of it, and because the potential is so devastating, a usual response from some people is, "Gee, why are you giving our potential enemies ideas?"

I just want to assure you that that's not happening.

I have a series of visuals in the Russia language detailing all of the effects of EMP. It's very well-known. As a matter of fact, EMP is an inadvertent compound of any nuclear explosion above the atmosphere. You can build bombs to enhance that. The Russians have done that. We designed them, but we never built them. The Russians have built and do have bombs to enhance EMP capability.

Several years ago, there was a major article in the New York Times on EMP. So the whole world could know it if the whole world read the New York Times. Tom Clancy—much of the world reads his books. There was a major EMP scenario in one of Tom Clancy's books.

In a little miniseries on television about 30 years ago when the Soviet Union took over this country called Amerika, A-M-E-R-I-K-A—most of you are too young to remember that, probably. But an EMP attack was a part of that.

Now, this is small. Because you can do the same thing with directed energy and hit a smaller target.

Just in the last day or two or so, there was a TV program that showed directed energy shutting down the infrastructure—in Las Vegas, was it, so they can rob the banks? So it's not like this is unknown. It really is known.

Let me give you some idea as to the Russia thinking. First of all, under the original Ballistic Missile Defense Treaty, the Russians could have put in place a system—we could have, too. We chose not to because it was North Dakota to protect by a launching missile silo. We chose not to do that because it wouldn't protect any of our people. Almost nobody lives in North Dakota. There's only one Congressman from all of North Dakota, for instance.

But the Russians have one, and it's around Moscow, and they have at least 100 interceptors that are nuclear tipped, and they can protect about 60–70 percent of all their people.

Starting in the days of Breshnev under a mountain called Yamata Mountain in the Urals supported by two closed cities—now, a closed city is a city that the tourists don't visit and those people don't go much of anywhere—two closed cities called Mishgorva, housing 60,000 people—the Russians have—the Soviets first and now the Russians continue—have spent $6 billion on the world's largest underground nuclear secure facility.

We do not know what it's there for. All we have is intelligence from at least two people who have defected. Highly, highly guarded secret. It doesn't appear on any of the ministries as a line item in terms of expenditures. It's only possible use is during or post nuclear war.

It's more important to the Russians because they are now building soccer fields there. When they can't pay their military officers and they didn't have $200 million for the service module on the international space station, they still had money to power into Yamata Mountain.

The Russians apparently believe that a nuclear war is inevitable and winnable and they're going to win it. They span 11 time zones. They go nearly halfway around the world, a very large country, with only six cities, I understand, of more than a million people and very little infrastructure in terms of how much we are dependent on infrastructure.

I hope the probability of this happening is very low, but also the probability of my home burning is very low. And I don't lay awake every night worrying about my home burning. I don't have a guard stationed there to yell, "Fire! Fire!" if one breaks out and I don't have a fire engine parked out front. But have done the prudent thing and I have bought an insurance policy. So if this very low probability, high impact event should occur, I'm going to have some protection.

Now, my question to you is and I would appreciate a response for the record, because I know that you haven't been thinking about this very much at all—but I would like to know what, in your view, is a reasonable insurance policy for us to buy?

You know, the unthinkable is not necessarily the impossible. Flying a plane load of 200-and-some people into a building was unthinkable before September 11. It sure as heck wasn't impossible. So the unthinkable is not impossible.

What would be a reasonable insurance policy, a reasonable investment for us to make in an insurance policy?

Because you haven't thought about that and because our time is up, I would be very appreciative if you could indicate that for the record because we would really like that.

The great wisdom of the country, by the way, is outside the beltway, so thank you, Mr. Chairman, for taking this hearing outside the beltway. I appreciate that in advance.

Thank you very much, Mr. Chairman, and thank you for your testimony and I would thank you in advance for your response to my question.

Mr. WEAVER. Weapons of mass destruction, is what we're talking about, and what's reasonable? I mean even the whole subject is not reasonable to most people.

The way we look at things is due diligence and best practices; and so when you look at what is good business and what is too much and what is too little and what the communities and the business people will accept and what the government is going to provide in homeland defense and homeland security and you start talking about electronic magnetic pulse and high energy radio frequency guns, HERF guns, and surviving nuclear holocaust and Armageddon, conventional attacks on top of other first responder attacks—attacking the first responders and dirty bombs; and where do we see ourselves inserting government as reasonable, as what's livable?

I don't know if anyone has all the answers to that, but it's a huge problem.

And we are in war right now. It doesn't look like it, doesn't feel like it, but I will tell you, I have seen hell on Earth. And whatever allowed that to happen can't continue.

And so I think it is reasonable to restructure and do things that will prevent that.

You must have heard many things about the shadow government and the second government. So I think that these are reasonable precautions.

We should have distributed networks. We shouldn't have all our eggs in one basket.

If anybody is going to survive, I would like to think that this country would do that and would survive, and that would be a reasonable thing for us to do.

It takes much greater thought than I have time to give it, but I would like to follow up on that with you, if we may.

Chairman BOEHLERT. By all means.

Dr. SHAMASH. I think raising the awareness I think is probably important also and making sure that we are continuing to do the basic research that we would need. I think that's a very good insurance policy for us, whether it's the National Science Foundation or the National Security Agency or somebody, but I think building up our research infrastructure to address that issue is important.

Mr. MIRAVALLE. This isn't a subject I have thought about and certainly I'm not qualified on the nuclear EMP scale responder.

I would offer this, though. If you look at the nuclear arms race from its inception, the premise was, you may hurt us but we're going to hurt you a lot worse. If you start it, we'll finish it. Of course, being from the same generation, we all grew up with that threat hanging over our heads.

The irony is now it's all controlled by computers. This hearing and our business that we're all about is, "How do we protect our nation's infrastructure from attack?" And I say, "Reverse the model." What's a good defense is equally good to attack with.

Maybe we're going to start the next cold war, the cyber cold war. You shut down our communication or power grid system, we're going to totally paralyze your country, assuming it's a civilized nation dependent on technology.

I would suspect in your scenario with the Russians, although their technology is somewhat more EMP hardened, as I'm sure you are all aware, particularly in their fighter aircraft, they are still very susceptible. There are still computer-based operations. That's what's going to launch that missile, anyway. Take down their infrastructure.

Mr. BARTLETT. But much of their domestic infrastructure is not nearly as dependent as ours.

Mr. MIRAVALLE. That's correct. That's correct.

Chairman BOEHLERT. Mr. Miravalle, that is a perfect epitaph for this meeting.

Mr. SMITH. "Epitaph," maybe you ought not use that word.

Chairman BOEHLERT. We started out emphasizing how important research and development is in the area of cyberspace. We have heard from expert witnesses telling us that we need to do more. We've heard from others who have said that there are deficiencies in our existing systems and our universities, and we need more exchange of information between government and the private sector.

I think this has been a very valuable hearing, and I would point out to the audience that each of the witnesses have a much more comprehensive statement of testimony than you have heard from here. We usually—at hearings in Washington, you know, we restrict it to a 5-minute summary. Today, we did a 10-minute summary, because I think it's more important that we hear some more from you and stimulate some additional questions from us.

But I think this has been a very productive hearing and now, Dr. Bartlett, I know he is going to be excited when he accompanies us up to the facilities. He is a Ph.D. You probably could discern that from the manner in which he was posing those questions. We are looking forward to a very exciting visit, a very rewarding visit with Mr. Urtz and his team up at the Rome research site.

It's a great place to visit. It's a great place to have your batteries recharged and feel good about a lot of good things that are being accomplished with Federal dollars and resources in our laboratories and the outreach program we have to the private sector.

So I thank all of you for being resources for this committee. I thank my colleagues for coming from Texas and Michigan and Maryland, and I thank all of you for evidencing your interest in the important work we're about.

The hearing is adjourned.

[Applause.]

[Whereupon, at 12 noon, the hearing was adjourned.]

APEX
TP
9780160696770
76901945—53